They said
I couldn't.
So I did.

A CIP catalogue of this book is available from the National Library of Australia.

Messenger, Lisa
Money & Mindfulness: Living in Abundance
ISBN 978-0-9943109-2-7

First published in 2015 by The Messenger Group Pty Ltd
PO Box H241
Australia Square NSW 1215

Editing: Amy Molloy and Mel Carswell
Proofreaders: Jen Taylor, Rebecca Hanley
Production Manager: Jade Dunwoody
Book design: Edith Swan
Photography of Lisa: Scott Ehler
Styling of Lisa: Jules Sebastian
Styling Assistant: Adam Cubito
Hair and make-up: Georgia Skye
Clothing: Pages 11, 22, 33, 157, 200, Top – Little Joe Woman by Gail Elliott, Shorts – South of the Boarder, Accessories – Thomas Sabo & Pierre Winter Fine Jewels. Pages 72, 77, 106, Top - Rolla, Jeans – A Brand. Page 97, Dress & Necklace – Ixiah. Pages 43, Top & Skirt – Manning Cartell. Pages 138, 128, 192, Cardi – Two Birds Talking PR, Accessories – Thomas Sabo & Pierre Winter Fine Jewels, Cami & Shorts – South of the Boarder, Uggs – (Lisa's own that she insisted on wearing). Pages 18, 87, 152, 162, 181, 196, Cardi & Dress – South of the Boarder, Cuff – Pierre Winter Fine Jewels. Page 54 Dress – Denisse M Vera, Hat – Third Stone.
PR Manager: Jessica Stones, jessica@collectivehub.com
Distribution enquiries: Claire Belbeck, claire@collectivehub.com

This is proudly a Collective product
collectivehub.com

DISCLAIMER
The content of this book is to serve as a general overview of matters of interest and is not intended to be comprehensive, nor does it constitute financial (or other) advice in any way. This book is a compilation of one person's ideas, concepts, ideologies, philosophies and opinions. You should carry out your own research and/or seek your own professional advice before acting or relying on any of the information displayed in this book. The author, Messenger Group Pty Ltd and its related entities will not be liable for any loss or damage (financial or otherwise) that may arise out of your improper use of, or reliance on, the content of this book. You accept sole responsibility of the outcomes if you choose to adopt and/or use the ideas, concepts, ideologies, philosophies and opinions within the content of this book.

Money + Mindfulness

Living in Abundance

Contents

It was a must to have this photo shoot at the beach — the place that always grounds me and where any worries are always washed away.

Introduction

I couldn't care less about money. You probably weren't expecting that opening line, but in all honesty, it's the truth… I couldn't care less about money for money's sake. I do, however, care about money for a host of other reasons. I don't want or need big, fancy things nor have I ever craved a super-duper, overflowing bank account. BUT, and it's a very big 'but', I have discovered that money buys you freedom, choice and, more often than not, a platform to make a difference in the world. For me personally, money is a means to fill my life with positive experiences – and to extend that positivity to people I love and the inspiring community growing around myself and *The Collective*.

So, with that in mind, I'm here to say it's okay to allow money to be a driving force in your life. And, that I now LOVE the potential power of money in all of our lives. Oh my goodness I do! Did I really just say that? Yes, I did. I love money, not because I dream of having a driveway full of fast cars and a closet full of designer outfits (I am 'stuffocating' at the very thought of it) but because the moment I stopped seeing money as the root of all evil and saw it as a fuel of fulfilment, everything changed for me – and I believe it can for you too. With it, you and I have the means to make a massive, life-altering, kick-arse difference in the world and that is one thing I won't budge on. I want to live a life of worth and of significance and I have discovered that money is a key ingredient in having the opportunities, choice and means to achieve that dream.

This is why I'm now an unapologetic oversharer when it comes to money and why, over the next few chapters, I will talk with raw honesty about my journey. I'll talk figures: like my plan to have revenue of AU$50 million in the next two years. I'll talk mistakes: we once printed the wrong date in a book that cost us AU$10,000 and a staff member and I had to sort it out over Christmas while I had the worst food poisoning of my life. I'll talk about learned strategies: finding money in places it apparently doesn't exist (loans, crowdfunding and venture capital are not routes I have taken, but I have found money in unlikely places through partnerships and sponsorship). And, more importantly, I'll talk about how our money mindsets and attitudes can affect our chances of succeeding.

I actually failed accounting (dismally) during my first attempt at university. I had to 'break up' with my accountant for four months when I launched *The Collective* and have, without a doubt, made my share of monetary mistakes, although none were fatal. I certainly wasn't a 'numbers girl' in the beginning, nor do I spruik that as my best asset today. But, what I have been able to do is keep my business, run across multiple industries, in the black – through the rocky seasons and on the tough financial days. Fourteen years from its start, my latest and most successful business venture – Collective Hub – includes a print magazine sold in more than 37 countries and over 3500 newsagents in Australia alone. I employ a staff of roughly 20 and a team of over 70 freelance creatives, and my personal favourite – I have holidayed on Necker Island with Sir Richard Branson. Collective Hub has led to brand extensions, including products, books, paid speaking events and consultancy meetings. I have achieved my business "success" (because I am certainly not there yet) with absolutely no outside investment or equity partners, other than some broad-minded thinking that led to sponsorship and advertising deals, and at the time of writing, every cent channelled into this business has been my own.

I'm guessing you picked up this book because you want more money in your life, you'd like to overcome your business cashflow woes, you want to attract funding to your idea or perhaps you'd like to look at money from a different angle. I am so glad you did, because it means you aren't planning on being a "gunna". At every event or every speaking gig I attend, I always meet at least one person who falls into a category that I call the "gunnas". These are the people who have huge dreams, wonderful visions, extraordinary potential and genuinely with all their hearts want to follow in the footsteps of entrepreneurs they admire. However, they are full of excuses about why it's not within their reach: "I'm unsure where to start", "I wish I was confident like you" or this one, "But it's okay for you, you probably come from a wealthy background." I always laugh when people say that because 14 years ago, when I began my first start-up, even the term 'shoestring' was exaggerating my resources. My finances were more comparable to dental floss. I could have been a "gunna" quite easily, making every justification not to follow my purpose because I didn't (at that point) have the means available at all. Instead, I decided to look at money differently, bring some fresh ideas to the table and try new things to succeed. I truly believe my naivety has worked to my advantage in a sense, because I've had to follow my intuition, trust my gut, learn to think outside the norm, challenge the status quo and find imaginative and unusual ways to build a castle from rubble. I believe I have discovered a personal formula for finding profit in the unprofitable, for stretching my means to pursue my dreams, and for living the fullest version of my life.

Over the years I have discovered processes, strategies and people that help me to amplify, expand and utilise the resources I have, to plug the gaps in my knowledge and lift me over any mental hurdles. And now, I'm happy to share it with you. What's more, I feel like I NEED to, because I truly believe the only way that we can all collectively rise up as a community is to stop seeing money as a dirty word and to talk about it – loudly and honestly.

I fully appreciate the M-word brings up mixed feelings in most people, including myself. Perhaps you almost didn't buy this book because it had the word "money" on the cover. Money, politics, sex and religion... Gulp! My generation was certainly raised to believe these topics were taboo and shouldn't be discussed lightly – or at all – even with your closest friends. Thankfully times have changed, but even at dinner parties today, I'll see people recoil as the subject arises. If that's the case for you, I'm sorry because I may just offend you. I want to talk about it loudly and unashamedly.

This is the book I wish I'd been given in my twenties when I'd look at my older, wiser friends who were buying houses and starting businesses and think – how on earth can they afford to do that? It's the book I wish someone gave me on my very first day in business or the book I wish someone had slipped into my bag at one of those networking events when people would talk about their success while in the back of my mind, I still wondered if I could make rent that week. I couldn't understand how anyone could afford to 'live life and prosper'. I was utterly desperate to know their secret. Did I ask them? Of course not! That was far too embarrassing and also would have been seen as bad manners. But inside, I secretly longed for answers and for many, many years I continued to tread water, unsure of where to go, what to do or how to approach the subject, until a fateful intervention from the universe (more on that later).

This is not a how-to book. There are some tips and tricks in here, but this is ultimately a book about my journey with money and how I've come to embrace it and positively want it. I'm no different to you, I'm just a businesswoman trying to make a mark on this world. However, I'm not averse to taking risks or backing myself, and when others would have probably retreated against hard financial times, I only fought harder. People say they don't have the money to create a start-up and I say, "f**k me, I didn't either!" And that's the point of this book. Somehow because of my attitude, ideas and approach to business, I managed to keep going and fund an incredible business that is now being taken seriously across the globe. I hope to bring fresh ideas and a bit of attitude to the table through these pages, to help you get your head in the right space to overcome your money fears or discover any internal blockages.

Think of this book as a blank cheque for your future (one of those massive ones they give out on *The Ellen DeGeneres Show* if that helps with your visioning). It's really up to you how you spend it, but just know it's yours if you want to take it. Reach out, grab it. Why don't you take a moment to visualise your future... with money in it. Whether you're an entrepreneur with a team of 50, a mother of a young family, the boss of a global corporation, or a single 20-something in the middle of an around-the-world adventure, I hope this book helps you examine your current thinking, appreciate your real value, amplify your self-worth and find the means to achieve everything you dream of.

It's time that those of us in the know stopped keeping our cards (gold or otherwise) so close to our chests, and spark honest, open conversations about money and how to make just enough to achieve your personal purpose and leave a rich, abundant legacy. I will never wake up with dollar signs in my eyes, but I do want to live a life so full of wonder, adventure and excitement, that when I look up at the night sky it seems full of diamonds. Who's with me?

I don't like money for money's sake, but money buys you freedom and choice.

Chapter 1

Money + Mentality

I was brought up in the day of hire purchases and lay-bys. Few people had credit cards back then, so you could really only spend what you could afford (yeah, that wouldn't fly in society today). My mum, a single parent, was paid in cash for her wages and I was always aware that money was a tough subject. As a result, there was a constant hovering, hindering worry that we didn't have enough, or quite as much as other people. I distinctly remember Mum sticking notes above the toilet paper roll saying something like, "just take one sheet" and feeling guilt-ridden if I 'indulged' by using two. (Although she now says that note was for environmental reasons, but the jury's out. Either way – go Mum!) As a kid, I viewed money – and how to earn it – with a mixture of fear, suspicion and superstition. I was the little girl parroting, "Find a penny, pick it up, all day long you'll have good luck," and I really believed it.

Fast-forward to my adult life and I still can't walk past a 5-cent coin on the pavement without bending down to pocket it. If you spotted me doing this, would you ever imagine that I'm actually the owner of a global business, the founder of a magazine sold in more than 37 countries – which costs over AU$350,000 an issue to produce – with multiple side projects, collaborations, partnerships and deals worth millions upon millions of dollars coming in every year? Yet, I still can't walk past a "penny". And that's not the only childhood imprint that has stuck with me as an adult.

A report authored by behaviour experts at Cambridge University found that an adult's attitude towards money is essentially formed by the age of seven. Seven! That means we're clued in on money matters probably long before sex, drugs, rock 'n' roll, politics and all those other 'evils' are on our childish radars. A 2014 survey by Halifax bank in the UK found that 77 per cent of children aged eight to 15 know their parents worry about money, close to the real figure of 91 per cent of parents who are actually concerned. The same study found that 59 per cent of children would like to learn about finance from their parents, followed by teachers at school (20 per cent), then the Internet (8 per cent) and television programs (4 per cent).

As an entrepreneur, everywhere I look – business meetings, networking events and social occasions – I can see glaring examples of grown-ups whose inner child still holds their purse strings. These grown-ups may as well be carrying Hello Kitty purses and handing out Monopoly money, because it's so obvious their early money memories still propel, control, enable or restrict them. I see it in the millionaire who doesn't like tipping, in the struggling freelancer who spends $2000 on a present, in the CEO who boasts about their profit but won't spend $10 on a magazine, and the start-up founder who honestly can't tell you how much his company is worth because he has zero grasp of the finances, so adopts a head-in-sand approach to business.

That is why, although this book is focused on helping you reach your full financial potential as an adult, I'm beginning chapter one by jumping into a time machine to revisit my childhood – and why I'm asking you to regress with me. Take a moment to think: what is your earliest money memory? How was money discussed in your household and how did it shape your view of the world, your parents, your peers, your neighbours and yourself?

You might look at me now and think I'm financially savvy, but it certainly hasn't always been this way. For many, many years I was scared of making money, losing money, saving money, spending money and deserving money. I was trapped in a mindset of scarcity where I had a warped view of wealth, how much I needed, how much I deserved and what I needed to do to achieve it. It took a lot of work, self-development and self-analysis to get to a point where I see money not as the enemy, but as an ally to help me achieve my purpose.

When I called my mother to ask about my financial upbringing before sitting down to write this chapter, she admitted that when my sister and I were little she did feel like a black cloud of worry was hanging over us. Just to put my own childhood into perspective, we were far from poverty-stricken. In fact, after our country upbringing in our pre-teen years, if we hadn't been raised in Sydney's affluent eastern suburbs and instead had a house in the deep west of the city, we probably would have been the richest in our neighbourhood. As it happens, we were definitely some of the poorest kids in a private school, the smallest house on the best street, the lowest percentile in a high percentage. Yet, as a single parent, my kind and sensitive mama was terrified of getting sick and not being able to support us, was adamant that she didn't want to take any handouts from family, and felt weighed down by financial responsibility. Even if I didn't realise it at the time, this does have a knock-on effect when you're an impressionable kid, and money became the monster under our beds, a dirty word we shouldn't mention and something that, for many years, I personally felt I didn't deserve.

I don't think I'm the only child to be raised around such fears, often by no fault of the parent who was just trying to do their best with the resources they had (while dealing with their own money memories passed down by their own parents, our grandparents, who have their own money memories passed down from our great-grandparents and so on). Even if you had a blissful childhood where money was abundant, it can still warp your perception of money in adulthood.

I remember watching a hilarious skit that the New Zealand comedy duo Flight of the Conchords recorded for Red Nose Day a few years ago called, 'Feel Inside (and Stuff Like That)'. They sat down with schoolchildren and asked them, among other things, about the economy. How much is a lot of money? Answers ranged from "a million" to "10" dollars and "your whole house full of money?" And, how do you make money? "We can get money from selling oil, gold and the crystals," replies one little girl, "I saw that in a movie I watched, *The Muppets*."

If you asked any child these questions, I'm sure you would get very different but equally cute answers. In a similar vein, Jeffrey Pritchard, an American

MONEY & MINDFULNESS

financial blogger, asked his seven-year-old daughter to answer some basic finance questions. What is money? "Change. And you could use it to buy stuff." How much money do you need to have to be considered rich? "Two thousand, ten hundred." What job do you want to do when you grow up and how much will it pay? "Farmer. Five dollars every day or every month." How much do you think a new house costs? "Ten thousand, fifty hundred." A car? "$548,060." At what age do people retire? "Probably 26."

However, all jokes aside, could these inaccurate perceptions have a lasting impression? Will these kids grow out of it? Will their ideas really shift, change and evolve as they age? Or do many of the associations we place around money as a child actually stick with us, like a secret fear of the dark, the belief that if we step on a crack it might break our mother's back, and an aversion to the taste of olives, though you haven't let one pass your lips since your older sister force-fed one to you in pre-school?

Don't be fooled into thinking your relationship with money began the day you cashed your first pay cheque, because I firmly believe that our attitude to money is deeply ingrained in us from our earliest experiences – when those mystical gold and silver coins that can be exchanged for lollies and marbles suddenly become a source of excitement, disappointment, terror or resentment, depending on the expression on a parent's face as they gaze at the number that flashes up on an ATM screen. When we learn to cheer on Cinderella in her rags, to fear the Wicked Stepmother in her finery, when Robin Hood battled Prince John, and we're taught that wealth makes you selfish, mean and a 'baddy', whereas poverty is associated with the 'goodie' and the eventual winner. And when we chose, very early on, where we would sit on that moral scale.

In his book, *My Life and Work*, the great Henry Ford (now there's a man who knew how to build a brand) wrote, "We teach children to save their money. As an attempt to counteract thoughtless and selfish expenditure, that has a value. But it is not positive; it does not lead the child out into the safe and useful avenues

You can never cross the ocean until you have the courage to lose sight of the shore.

— Christopher Columbus

of self-expression or self-expenditure. To teach a child to invest and use is better than to teach him to save."

I learned a lot of long-lasting lessons during my childhood that had both positive and negative connotations – money is scarce, you shouldn't take it for granted and the need to budget strictly. The same lessons that have allowed me to grow a business out of nothing have also nearly broken me, and for a long time stopped me living as the fullest version of myself because I refused to invest in myself, back myself, enable myself or ask for what I was owed.

I am not here to tell you to wipe your mind of all childhood associations (if only it was that easy!) but to examine your attitude to money, which associations are working for you and which are self-sabotaging. I hope that I never, ever stop picking 5-cent coins up off the street, even if I become a multibillionaire, because it is that jingle of coins in my pocket, the superstitious belief that money can bring magic, which continues to drive me, to ground me, motivate me and inspire me. (Side note: a friend of mine in America told me recently that a few weeks ago, he found 13 cents in the street and picked it up, much to the amusement of a passer-by walking near him. At the time, money was on his mind because he needed a plane ticket home to Australia but couldn't afford one. A few days later he was taking a domestic flight across America and the airline had overbooked the flight and offered anyone who was prepared to stay a day and get the flight tomorrow US$1300 as compensation. Can you believe it? So this US$1300 paid for his ticket back to Australia. The universe works in mysterious and wonderful ways if you stay open to it. It is that reminder that money can be lost and found so instantly, which stops me becoming too attached to it, ensures I remember that wealth is subjective and fleeting, can grace anyone's palm and burn a hole in anyone's pocket.)

I recently watched a TED talk by Tania Luna, an entrepreneur originally from the Ukraine, who left her hometown with her family after Chernobyl to take asylum in America. In the talk, she recalls living in a homeless shelter ("We think that it's a hotel – a hotel with lots of rats") and the moment she and her sister, as schoolgirls, discovered true treasure in the street. "So, we find this penny kind of fossilised in the floor and we think that a very wealthy man must have left it there because regular people don't just lose money," says Tania, "And I hold this penny in the palm of my hand and it's sticky and rusty but it feels like I'm holding a fortune. I decide that I'm going to get my very own piece of Bazooka bubble gum. And in that moment I feel like a millionaire."

These are the kind of childhood lessons that should never be forgotten, that we should lock up in a safe and pass down to our children with their inheritance. I'll never forget the sense of pride when I cashed my first pay cheque shortly after my 15th birthday, as a proud employee of KFC, where I just remember sliding across the floor at the end of a shift like an ice-skater in my white plastic shoes, complete with the deep satisfaction of tucking into leftover chips dipped in potato and gravy on the walk home. However, I also have to check myself when I am tortured with guilt over spending $2 on a bottle of water, when I'm tempted to undercharge a client or want to avoid my accountant's phone calls. I have to stop and ask – where are these fears coming from? Are they based on fact or is there another factor at play?

Don't place a price tag on your ambitions because dreams find the means.

GET CLEAR ON THINGS

To make enough money (and 'enough' will be a different value for everyone) it's so important to set clear, specific intentions. The day before writing this chapter, with money on my mind, I sat down with three of my senior team members to set our financial goals for the next year. As we lazed on sun lounges besides the pool at a lovely Sydney hotel, sipping on a smoothie (because for me, sun + water + good food + fresh air = inspiration), I jotted down figures in a notebook – and they were very specific. "I want AU$20 million in revenue in the next financial year from these specific revenue streams…" I realise that sounds like a lot to some and a little to others. Remember, at the time of writing this book *The Collective* was only two years old… everything is always relative.

I believe that it's extremely important to set concrete parameters. Once you know exactly what you want and you quantify it with a dollar amount, a time frame, where it is coming from and what it will be used for, it is very hard to stop it from happening. I read a book years ago titled *I Could Do Anything If Only I Knew What It Was*. I don't remember any of the contents (and to be honest I don't know if I even read the book or just the blurb) but the title stuck with me. I truly believe that once we know exactly what we want, the universe delivers every single time without fail (even if the road is a little windy or if we get a bit lost along the way). It's the getting clear on exactly what it is that we want that is the tricky part.

I am a big believer in the power of visioning, whether it's imagining the relationship you want, the work culture you'd like to be a part of, or how much money your future-self has in their bank account. A lot of people make the mistake when visioning of being far too airy-fairy: "I just want to be a millionaire" or "I just want to be rich" – but what does this really mean to you? How much do you need to be happy and fulfil your life purpose?

I know the exact yearly income that I could very comfortably live on (and I don't desire any more than that for personal use), and yet I want to make a hundred times that; well into the tens of millions, because I need to in order to expand and amplify my brand and my purpose – to use myself as a conduit to be an entrepreneur for entrepreneurs, to live my own life out loud so others can see it and hopefully, be inspired by it. This is why my visioning is very specific and why I recommend that you also pinpoint your own dream income, financial timeline and end goal. I'm not the only one who believes in this strategy; for years those in the know have been visioning in detail.

In 1937, in the depth of the Great Depression, a book called *Think and Grow Rich* became a bestseller. The author, Napoleon Hill, was a former advisor to President Franklin D Roosevelt and for the book, he interviewed more than 500 of the most successful men in the country to try and calculate the key to their good fortune. "Define the exact amount of money you desire," he writes. "It is not sufficient merely to say, 'I want plenty of money'. Be specific as to the amount."

He then recommends writing out your financial desire – including the time limit for its acquisition – and reading it aloud twice a day, once just before waking up and once just before going to sleep. "As you read, see and feel and believe in yourself already in possession of the money," he writes. I've tried it, and I highly recommend it. Yes, you will feel like a lunatic at first, but I can vouch that this type of pillow talk is profitable. Another key point is to get clear on what you will give in return for the money, as he said, "There is no such thing as something for nothing." That book went on to sell over 70 million copies worldwide. Clearly, there has to be some truth in it. So, today set your intention and tomorrow repeat it aloud, then repeat it again the next day and the next until you hit that milestone, at which point, celebrate wildly and then it's time to upgrade and expand your intentions even further. This isn't about relying on a prayer or believing in a higher power. It's about sending a clear, concise message to yourself and imagining a solid casino chip in your palm that you can see, feel and touch – and one day cash in.

Chapter 2

Hurdles + Hang-Ups

When I launched my book publishing business around 11 years ago, I'll never forget the delicious thrill of signing our very first client. It felt like Christmas morning when you're a kid, combined with your first crush as a teenager and the first time you hear "I love you" as an adult. I was just sooooo excited that someone actually wanted to hire my services (they like me, they really like me!) that I didn't think about the practicalities – like charging them appropriately. I was so amazed that my dream was happening, that my commercial mindset (what little there was at the time) went out the window. I would have happily done the project for free. Hell, I would have paid them to hire me.

And so for a project that took 13 months to complete, I charged just AU$4000, which definitely wasn't nothing, but was it profitable? I could have earned more selling homemade lemonade from a crate outside my office. At an average of 20 hours of manpower per week, the project would have taken a total of 1040 hours, which meant our hourly rate was about AU$3.85. Meanwhile, the client made about AU$195,000 in revenue – and he was still late in paying me.

Yet, I can't blame the client (although I'm gritting my teeth writing this) because he didn't ask for such a low fee – I naively offered it! If I had to sum up the first three years of my business in two words they would be, 'overservicing' and 'undercharging'. I was working around the clock to offer the best service at the lowest possible cost, totally underestimating my own worth and that of my company. Most start-ups struggle because they can't get attention or find clients, yet people were falling over themselves to work with us (and I'm so grateful, as I look back on that time). But in the end, it was more than just because of what we did: we represented a phenomenal bargain and as a result, people utterly loved us.

In those early days we didn't charge any mark-up on costs. Not a cent! When it came to production of the books, we handed the invoice totals straight from the manufacturers to our clients. We didn't even charge an administration fee. Because I inherited my grandfather's stoic work ethic (he was an Australian politician and was up working before sunrise and still going well after dark every day, actively involved in charity, on the board of many prominent organisations and playing tennis until nearly the day he died), I went over and beyond on every project and also wanted to treat all of our clients like VIPs no matter what they could offer us. This is exactly why, on one memorable occasion, I ended up being held to ransom on a trampoline at a client's launch party. After already losing money on the job, I should have said no when she asked me to MC her launch party for free (I didn't). I should have also walked away when she got extremely drunk at the party and expected me to spend three hours on her son's trampoline with her (again, I didn't). It was a lesson in boundaries – and a lack of them.

This brings me to this chapter's topic: hurdles and hang-ups. Because even the most eager and experienced entrepreneur can get caught out, hung-up and held back by money memories, imprints and scars from their past, like those we discussed in chapter one.

There is a reason that so many financial planners are teaming up with life coaches, psychologists and counsellors – because helping a person become financially prosperous isn't simply about teaching them how to calculate profit margins. I recently read an article where financial planners estimated they spent 25 per cent of their time with clients talking about non-financial issues, such as family dysfunction, illness, divorce, depression or spirituality. They really should think about putting therapist's couches in bank manager's offices (I'm only half joking) because of the layer upon layer of emotional barriers, roadblocks and hurdles that affect whether a person can balance a bottom line. Have you ever said the sentence, "I'm not good with money"? What does that really mean? What is at the crux of that statement? Do you mean you're not good at maths, multiplying and square-rooting or does the problem run much deeper? I'd hedge a guess that it's not simply a matter of not understanding taxable income.

Do you suffer from low financial self-esteem? I certainly did. At this early stage of my entrepreneurial journey, I didn't have the insight to see how my childhood memories and my subconscious belief that money could cause trouble, upset and envy, were affecting how I handled my business in adulthood. When it came to my assets, I was blinkered to my real worth and I was afraid to ask for what I deserved because I didn't want to admit that money does actually matter. With the wisdom of experience, I should have sat down with that first client and laid out exactly how much manpower the project would take, how much to-and-fro we would do with the production team, and the discounts I would be able to pass on because I'd nurtured relationships with suppliers. I should have explained that this is what he was paying for – the abstract skills that aren't always visible – our intellectual property, our connections and relationships, our experience, as well as the manpower and the materials. I only had myself to blame because I bit my lip and blocked my own profit. I didn't feel worthy. Clearly, I didn't yet value myself. But the problem with being a financial people-pleaser is the more you do for other people, the more they expect, for even less, and so you embark on a steep downwards spiral, which eventually leads to resentment.

I think the only reason my business didn't go under in those early days was because we had a huge number of projects on the go at once with a constant flow of cash and low overheads – it was just me and one other staff member working on them (Mel is now my deputy editor at *The Collective*, so she's obviously forgiven me for nearly driving her to a breakdown). My biggest problem was I set absolutely no boundaries. Mel still tells the story of the time a client rang her at one o'clock in the morning. A naked Mel leapt out of bed thinking there was an emergency and sat on the stairs outside of her bedroom talking to him, so as not to wake her sleeping husband. What was the emergency? He wanted to change the colour of the font on his book cover. Seriously! She says she caught a glimpse of herself in a mirror and thought,

"What the hell am I doing?" She really is the employee of the century.

I kept convincing myself that I loved what I was doing so much, and that I was so lucky to be running my own business, that it didn't matter what I was charging. I kept convincing my staff (and by 'staff' I mean Mel) that it really didn't matter that we were a smidge broke (I was driving a Mazda 121 that you could only get in and out of via the window and Mel and I shared a phone – she would put people on hold with her hand instead of a hold button because we didn't have the funds to get a proper phone system). The world was ours! We would never go hungry because our bellies were full of passion and ambition. Right? Wrong, Lisa, very wrong!

In my case, I had fallen into the trap of mistakenly believing that my passion could replace the need for profit – and I don't think I'm the only budding entrepreneur to do this. Think about it: when most start-up founders embark on an adventure, it's generally because they've fallen head-over-heels in love with a project, a product or a good cause. They're driven by the belief they can make a real difference, and often the relief at escaping cubicle life in a big corporation.

As for me, three years after starting the business of my dreams, I had reached a point of total resentment. If I'm honest, I just wanted to say a great big "f**k you" to all my clients, even the ones I loved. I wanted to scream as they walked out of my office, "I'm getting paid practically nothing and you don't seem to care!"

I can say without doubt that if I'd continued in this way, there is no way my business would still be standing, and certainly no way I'd be holding myself up as a good example. So, what changed? Well, those of you who've read my previous book *Daring & Disruptive* may remember me talking about a seminar I went to, which I paid AU$1200 to attend (despite the fact I was so skint at the time I had trouble affording toothpaste).

The seminar was run by an incredible Australian motivational speaker and an expert on leadership, and it turned out to be one of the richest weekends of my life to date, in both the emotional and financial sense. From this man I learned the importance of valuing your time (at the time he charged AU$1000 an hour, worked for 120 days a year and spent the rest of the year with his family) but it was the other keynote speakers who also had a lasting effect on me. Their overt selling-from-the-stage tactics had me in knots and wanting to run the other way – it was so garish. Yes, you read that right. But they certainly had an impact.

That weekend a dozen or so keynote speakers took to the stage to lecture our group on how to make money and many were everything I didn't want this book to be – aggressive, egotistical, competitive, preying on other people's insecurities and desires. I'll never forget one speaker who stood on stage and announced something like, "Right, the first 20 people to run to the back of the room and hand me a cheque for AU$20,000 can fly to America and do a course with me." I was glued to my seat but you should have seen people running, pushing and shoving to get their spot.

Yet, for me, it was the best thing I could have witnessed because it was such an extreme antithesis to my own mindset that it forced me to find my own happy medium. Okay, I definitely never wanted to be like that man on stage, selling his services in such a hideous manner, but I also quite liked the notion of making money. At least a little. At least what I deserved for my hard work. And just like that, I got hungry for change… and for cash.

Let me live.
let me breathe.

—Anonymous

MODESTY AND MISERY

I recently read a blog post that really resonated with me called 'The Myth of the Starving Artist'. It argued many people buy into a romantic notion that art is somehow more legitimate if its creator is a broke one. Just think of the struggling writer typing away on a dusty typewriter or – in the start-up world – the entrepreneur who uses their final $100 to launch their business and has to sleep on their friend's futon. There can be a certain glorification of destitution. We all love a 'rags to riches' story.

In the blog post, the writer uses the example of a "starving artist" he knows who makes handmade buttons at parties. For $3 he will come to your house, do a custom painting on a 1-inch canvas and then turn it into a button. All for less than a fiver! As business models go, it's utterly terrible – generous but flawed, unselfish but not at all sustainable. And yet, he is seen as a more "authentic" an artist for not chasing commercial gain.

Now, look at the opposite end of the artistic spectrum and the backlash creatives such as Damien Hirst and Andy Warhol have faced when they started selling their work for six-figure price tags. Okay, personally I'm not sure that I agree a painting of a vintage Coca-Cola sign is worth US$57.3 million, which is what Andy Warhol's 'Coca-Cola [3]' was sold for in late 2013, but I don't need to agree with it. The worth of that artwork is totally subjective, and if someone is willing to cough up that eye-watering sum, then why shouldn't the artist (or the artist's beneficiaries) accept it? Okay, the material used to produce it (casein on cotton) would have cost barely anything but factor in the talent, the time spent creating it, the brainstorming, not to mention the years upon years of networking and relationship-building that artists such as Andy Warhol had to endure to get noticed in the art world, long before he was considered acclaimed. Why shouldn't you take the money when the buyer willing to write the cheque obviously believes that it is worth it, either as an investment opportunity or because looking at it brings them so much pleasure?

Is it any wonder that so many of us undervalue our services when there's such a stigma around money – you don't want to look greedy, you don't want to be labelled a sell-out, you don't want to ruin your reputation. The Hollywood actor Dustin Hoffman didn't admit until he was well into his seventies that he actually co-wrote the screenplays for many of the famous films he acted in, including *Kramer vs. Kramer*. Why the modesty? He was worried people would think less of him. "There was a dignity to being a failure," says Dustin of his early days as an actor in New York. "If you were in a soap opera – or, God forbid, a commercial – you never admitted it. That was what was nice about being in the theatre – if you were unemployed, it meant you hadn't sold out."

We live in a discount-centric economy, with half-price sales, discount warehouses and posters in every shop window boasting they have the biggest savings. From the customer's point of view they hold more power than ever, but what about the knock-on effect for companies? Look at the recent wave of discount sites – at the end of quarter two in 2014, nearly 92 million customers had downloaded an app for one such website, so they could search for discounts. I'm sure the customers are grateful for the savings, but according to a story in *Forbes*, the merchants themselves usually lose money on the offers, which is why they usually use the websites as a way of attracting new customers rather than a medium for repeat campaigns.

A few years ago, a blog post written by a company owner who had regularly used a discount website went viral, after the café owner in Portland, US, called the discount campaigns, "the single worst decision I have ever made as a business owner thus far." Jessie Burke, the owner of Posies Bakery & Café, had offered a deal on Groupon where her customers could get US$13 worth of products for US$6. BUT – and here is the kicker – she agreed to give Groupon 50 per cent of the revenue for customers who signed up to this offer. Why would she do that? Well, she was convinced it would be good publicity, amplify her profile and that most customers would probably buy more once in her café. Obviously she needed more than half of her revenue to cover costs because she estimates that within three months, she'd lost US$10,000, which is no small amount for a budding business. Now, I've never used any such discount sites to push a product, so I'm not in a position to judge who they best serve, but looking on from the outside I do think it's an interesting quandary for a start-up to debate – and not sign up to without thorough deliberation.

In terms of boosting your profile, it clearly has a ton of positives and for that, these discount websites can be applauded. We all know customers love a bargain. We all love a bargain. Start-ups can fall into the trap of thinking some money is better than no money coming in, but from experience I've learned that this isn't actually accurate. And this is why I believe there is such a thing as being too modest with your margins. Think about it this way: if you were clearing out your garage and selling your unwanted stuff on Gumtree or Craigslist, if you could only get $50 for a bike, would it be worth the effort and your time to deal with potential buyers, the time-wasters who don't turn up or worse (in my opinion) having to arrange for a courier to deliver it to them, even if it was at their cost? Surely not. This is a simple example, but the principle still stands – we must value our time.

What if I fall?
Oh, but my darling
what if you fly?

—Erin Hanson

TALKING CHEAP

Are you pricing your products in a manner that is profitable for your small business, which will offer you a long-term future, and allow you to expand, prosper and thrive? Pretty much anyone with no business training could have a short-term one-hit wonder company, if they offered a product or service for a fifth of the price of their competitors. But, your company probably won't be around to celebrate its 10th anniversary – or even your second anniversary if we're being brutally honest. As American author Zig Ziglar says, "Money isn't the most important thing in life, but it's reasonably close to oxygen on the 'gotta have it' scale."

This was a home truth I had to face – and quickly. So, when I came back from that weekend seminar all those years ago, I upped my fees overnight. Just like that. I took back control. Now, I know I'm a 'back of the envelope' type gal but let me make one thing clear – I didn't just pluck a figure from the air. I sat down with a notepad and, over four hours, I logically, objectively and realistically wrote down how much work really went into our average projects. I looked at the margins other publishing companies added to their production costs (those that I was aware of) and theorised others. I thought realistically about how much I could shave off and calculated a fee that made us appear competitive without being mugs.

Of course, our new business model didn't go down well with everyone, especially returning clients who were used to hiring us in exchange for a pocketful of small change. However, in the new iteration of my company, I learned an important lesson in the power of 'no' and focusing on the long-term picture. We did lose some clients, but we soon picked up others who didn't think twice when we mentioned our fees. We went from potentially being the cheapest to being far from the cheapest, but I would certainly argue that we were absolutely the best at what we did and so I felt comfortable and authentic about stepping into this new model. As an aside, so ballsy did I become that I had banners and business cards made up with the slogan "Revolutionising the publishing industry globally". It was about 2006, approximately seven years before *The Collective* was born.

I heard an analogy about cars years ago that has stuck with me and guided me. There was a simple question: do you want to be a Lamborghini or an Audi? It wasn't a trick question – both are perfectly good cars, both service different markets, and both have become household names because of it. But you can't try to be both, you can't slap a Lamborghini price tag on an Audi and vice-versa, or try to convince your customers that you're one when you're actually the other. You need to choose where you want to sit in the market and then ensure that your messaging, which includes your marketing, your price tag and your promises, are consistent. In the instance of Lamborghini and Audi, they are two completely different business models. In 2013, Lamborghini brought out a new model with a price tag of US$4 million, building only three (which were bought by private buyers before they'd even set eyes on the finished product) in a quality-over-quantity business model, where customers aren't just buying a car but exclusivity, bragging rights and being part of a special club of elite owners. Yes, it's an ego-driven sale, but it's undoubtedly commercial for that end of the luxe market. And having driven one full-speed around a track in Vegas, I can certainly vouch for the hotness factor.

On a lesser scale, some people baulk that we charge AU$9.95 for one issue of *The Collective*, yet let's remember that magazine costs over AU$350,000 per issue just for us to produce. When a reader holds that magazine in their hands, they are benefitting from AU$280,000 per month in fixed staff and office running costs, plus AU$40,000 in writing and photography, then all sorts of other fees to do with contribution, distribution and consultations. They are holding a AU$350,000 baby in their hands. I purposefully priced the magazine at less than a tenner because it was my mission to build a community, not be hoity-toity or too exclusive, and we were relying on our readers' passion and loyalty to keep our circulation up so our sale price could be low. There are other magazines, especially in the UK and US markets, who opt for a different approach, bringing out one issue a year but pricing it extremely high and marketing themselves as a collectible artwork. Look at *Visionaire* magazine, whose 63rd issue retailed for US$350. It was printed on metal and they only produced 1500 numbered copies. That's a seriously pricey publication, but kudos to them for identifying a market, valuing and backing themselves. We now charge AU$200 for a mint-condition copy of our very first issue, because we don't have many left and it is in such short supply that it has become a more valuable commodity. Some of our readers see it as an investment they'd like in their collection. Simple economics of supply and demand.

It can take a lot of courage to price your worth in our bargain-hungry culture, especially if you're launching a new, groundbreaking or disruptive product or service and have little or nothing to benchmark it against. One entrepreneur I know says that when pricing a new product, he looks at its closest competitor and then adds a 20 per cent "innovation tax" to get to his RRP. "That covers the cost of all the sleepless nights, self-doubt and false starts that it takes to launch a brand new product," he says, and he has a good point.

In 1976, the first Apple-1 computer went on sale for a retail price of US$666.66, which was seen as controversially high by many. But Steve Wozniak argues this was a fair calculation when you factor in expertise, material and a little margin. The wholesale cost to stores was US$500, they added on a third to get the retail price to US$667, then rounded it down to US$666.66. "I was into repeating digits," explains Steve, adding it was "just easier to type".

In the business world, I firmly believe you get what you pay for. If you're offering an eye-wateringly low price, what are you saying about your standard of service? I recently spotted a quote on Instagram posted by Kelly Gregorio a writer for Advantage Capital Funds, the business finance incubator. It read, "Don't demoralise your efforts by setting rates that are beneath your results." These days, those are words I try to work by. As Oprah Winfrey says, "When you undervalue what you do, the world will undervalue who you are."

Another interesting point that I've heard from many experienced business owners is that while we assume customers want cheap-as-chips services, they can be suspicious if you sell yourself short. A client of mine did a very interesting experiment. They were selling Italian-made handbags for about AU$90, which was far cheaper than their competitors, and yet nobody was buying them. So they decided to do a test and hike the price up to AU$350. That's a 288 per cent price increase. Yet this reverse-sales tactic oddly worked and the exact same handbag started flying out the door. It was as if customers couldn't understand why they were so cheap before, and is a fascinating look at human psychology and our expectations, perceptions and suspicions.

That's not to say I always get it right. I still have moments everyday when I think, "sh*t, why didn't I charge more?" when I realise I've underestimated the effort a project will take to finish. But that happens less often these days and if it does, I don't beat myself up because I learn from the nuisance or twist presented by every single project. If I had to sum up this chapter it would be this: have faith in your product and have faith in yourself. If you tell people what you're offering is worth a certain amount and you honestly believe it is in your soul, they will believe it too.

those who don't
believe in *magic*
will never find it.

- Roald Dahl

A Money Meditation

As I mention in all of my books, I am a big fan of positive meditation and visualisation. It might sound at odds, mixing meditation and money (isn't one all about letting go and the other about getting?) but they actually mix together wonderfully, which is why when I was sitting down to write this chapter I asked the amazing life coach and motivational speaker Gabrielle Bernstein, who we were lucky enough to feature in an early issue of *The Collective*, to share her favourite money meditation from her book *Miracles Now*.

Pray Before You Pay
by Gabrielle Bernstein

"I have to admit that I used to be one of those people who let the bills pile up. Yup, I was that girl. Every month the stack on my desk grew bigger and wobblier. Every time I looked at it, I felt pangs of frustration over having to pay them. Maybe it stemmed from an old fear of not having enough, or maybe I was just exercising my self-sabotage muscles. Whatever the issue, it was a pretty awful monthly ritual.

Then it became clear that my bad habit was blocking me in many ways and creating unnecessary frustration and guilt. My bill pile was cluttering up my desk space – a real no-no. The ancient Chinese method of feng shui emphasises releasing all clutter in the office space. Clutter has a profound impact on our emotional, mental, physical and spiritual wellbeing. The value of clearing the clutter is that it releases vital energy that helps with mental clarity, inspiration and even our earning capacity!

So my first step towards healing my relationship with bills was to clear the clutter off my desk. I gathered my pile of bills and organised each statement in a beautiful green box. (If your bills are paperless, you can make a similar move with your email. Simply create coloured labels or folders for each bill and organise them as they come in, so you are never searching for the latest email statement.)

Once I was organised, I committed to bringing my spiritual practice to my monthly bills. I sat with my beautiful green box and prayed over each bill before cutting a cheque. I said, "Thank you, Universe, for providing me with the resources to pay these bills. I am grateful to contribute to the economy and to support my growing business."

Simply saying this prayer before paying each bill energised me. I was infused with an attitude of gratitude rather than an essence of anxiety and tension.

Now my bill-paying process is much more enjoyable and my desk is clutter-free. To top it all off, as soon as I cleared my desk space I started to notice many more career opportunities come through. Money began to flow more freely once I cleared the space to receive it.

If you're someone who experiences a lot of anxiety around paying bills, use these tips to bust through the block. Clear your desk and pray before you pay!"

Chapter 3

Time is Money

R emember when the supermodel Linda Evangelista famously said, "I don't get out of bed for less than $10,000 a day"? Wow, love her or hate her, that was a publicity coup (it's been called the most famous quote in fashion history, or the "let them eat cake" of the 21st century). But is it really that diva-ish a statement? This is a woman who clearly knew what people were willing to pay for her specific skill set and so, also knowing that a modelling career generally has an expiration date, wasn't prepared to waste a moment for less than her rate. If she'd been selling concrete, a tangible product rather then her skill set, would people have questioned it? Would you expect a Ferrari dealer to one day sell a car for $330,000 and the next day sell it for $50,000? In this day and age, time is one of our greatest commodities, and yet a lot of us give it away for free (or the price of a coffee).

Now, I am certainly no model (I hope you can hear me laughing from wherever you are), but Linda and I do have something in common. I now charge at least AU$10,000 for a speaking gig. I'M SORRY! Actually no, I'm not sorry, because that's truly what my time is worth these days, and part of the process of overcoming my money hang-ups is learning to accept that, and not to apologise for it.

Think of it this way: if I'm speaking for two hours at seminar, once you factor in travel time, question time and a bit of book signing, it can easily zap an entire day from of my schedule. If that day was spent at *The Collective* office, I could have held four or five partnership meetings, which if nailed, could bring in deals upwards of AU$100,000. Suddenly, my AU$10,000 personal price tag doesn't look so diva-ish (in fact, by the time you read this book, it may be even more, as my brand has hopefully grown and my personal currency has increased in relation).

Of course, there are always non-monetary trades and I talk about this a lot, but these do need to be value exchanges of equal value.

Many of us, whether we're business owners or employees, are guilty of undervaluing just how important, precious and valuable our time is. We all have just 525,949 minutes in a year and, taking into account that the average life expectancy is 84 for an Australian woman and 80 for an Australian man, that means we have around 44.7 million minutes in a lifetime. It might sound like a lot but if, like me, you have big plans, big dreams and a very deep bucket list, you need to use every second wisely – whether that is to achieve, rest, recover, play, laugh or pursue your purpose.

It was Steve Jobs who said, "My favourite things in life don't cost any money. It's really clear that the most precious resource we all have is time", which is even more poignant as he passed away before his 57th birthday. And so, here's the truth – you have to be a little selfish with your time, you have to protect it, guard it and value it for the irreplaceable resource that it is. What I've learned along the way is time is a resource that needs to be monitored like a bank balance.

If you want to have a sustainable, long-term business, to be productive, happy and healthy, it's imperative you see time as a commodity that has to be traded just like any other. Take it from someone who is far wiser than me: "It's a different kind of resource," says American psychologist Dr Alan Zimmerman of time. "You can't buy it, rent it, borrow it, store it, save it, renew it or multiply it. All you can do is spend it. And unlike other resources, such as talent, education or money, we all have the exact same amount of time. It's the only aspect of our lives where we are all truly equal."

WHAT IS YOUR PERSONAL PRICE TAG?

When it comes to time and its worth, one of my all-time favourite analogies was written by the French novelist Marc Levy, although I have no idea how I stumbled across this, as I haven't read any of his books (they're on my book bucket list).

"If you want to know the value of one year, just ask a student who failed a course.
If you want to know the value of one month, ask a mother who gave birth to a premature baby.
If you want to know the value of one hour, ask the lovers waiting to meet.
If you want to know the value of one minute, ask the person who just missed the bus.
If you want to know the value of one second, ask the person who just escaped death in a car accident.
And if you want to know the value of one-hundredth of a second, ask the athlete who won a silver medal in the Olympics."

I once quoted this to a dear friend who was widowed when she was young and she added her own heartbreaking version, "If you want to know what an hour is worth, just ask the wife who can't make it to a car crash in time to say goodbye to her husband." It's a sobering way to look at time, and my friend's words really stuck with me. How big does a block of time need to be before you place a value on it? Are you happy to work for 10 minutes for free? For an hour? For a day? For a month? For a year? It's all very simple for me to say I charge AU$10,000 for a full-day's speaking gig, but when it comes to time currency, every cent counts and it's also important not to undervalue the small segments as well.

I used to give way too much of my time away for free. I'd dole it out by the hour-load, handing it around like free candy, desperately trying to please people. When my business really began to take off, and my profile rose first in the publishing world and later on in the start-up sphere, I began to get emails from other entrepreneurs asking if they could pick my brains. "How do you do it? Can you help me?" For a while I tried to meet every Tom, Dick and Harry, for "quick coffees" that turned into two-hour therapy sessions, and "catch-ups" that became marathon brainstorms. Oh, everyone was very grateful, and I met some amazing people along the way, but all these little chinks in my day were not only affecting my productivity, they were also draining my energy and creative ideas, and consequently, hurting my own business.

Sometimes by the time I sat down with my own team I had no ideas left to give because I was intellectually exhausted, and I didn't have time to keep track of my own clients. I was so busy giving to strangers that I was starting to neglect my own purpose, my own team and my own clients.

I love the analogy that Arianna Huffington, who we were fortunate enough to interview in the early days of *The Collective*, uses to describe the reason she guards her time carefully to avoid burnout, and why – if her inbox is full – instead of rushing to answer emails she does a meditation exercise. "It pulls you out of automatic pilot," explains Arianna. "When you're on an airplane you're told to 'secure your own mask before helping others', even your own child. After all, it's not easy to help somebody else breathe easier if you're fighting for air yourself."

YES! Sorry to shout, but YES! I couldn't have put it better myself. This is why zapping your time, draining your resources, emptying your well to try and help others can – and probably will – become detrimental. If I burn out, if I put my health on the line because I'm trying to fit the workload of 68 hours into a 24-hour cycle, then my big dreams for the future, my big hopes for making a difference and the impact on the community we're building will not be possible. As I said in my book *Life & Love*, my hierarchy of priorities goes: #1 health, #2 family and friends and #3 my business, because without optimum wellness, no one can be a good companion or leader. That's why, a few years ago, I made probably one of the smartest decisions of my career.

I had to start seeing all these "quick coffees" for what they really are – consultations – and therefore charging for them, just as I would any product or service. So, I sat down and researched what other experts were charging and then I reduced it slightly (I might be commercially-minded, but I'm not greedy).

I set a rule that from that day onwards, I would charge AU$500 an hour to anyone who wanted to meet with me. Then I put measures in place so that I would go through with it. I am very aware that I find it hard to say no to people, so I put a 'gatekeeper' in place and removed myself from the conversations entirely. If any emails came in from people I hadn't met, asking if they could "pick my brains", I forwarded them straight on to a delegated team member who then kindly and politely informed them of my rates and said that I'd love to meet with them (which I genuinely did), but that it would have to be on a consultancy basis.

It was a decision that took a lot of courage on my part. I'll never forget my first ever AU$500 meeting, with a guy who was launching an outsourcing website (oh the irony!) and wanted to know how to get publicity. When he turned up at my office, which looked more like a friend's home, to be greeted by my dog Benny at the door and handed a latte freshly brewed by my 17-year-old staffer, I wondered what on earth he was thinking. "I paid AU$500 to meet her? She looks like a kid. She has a dog. There are pink textas on the boardroom table. Are you kidding me?" If only he knew that I swapped my Chucks for high heels as he knocked on the door. (Today, I'd just leave the Chucks on. Unlike Linda Evangelista, I do not have to be aesthetically perfect in the corporate sense of the word. I am not paid to look a certain way – I am paid because of how I think and that means I can look however I want – I think, anyway). Remember this was some years ago when the cool, tech start-up, pool-table-in-your-office and free-beer-on-tap kind of office hadn't taken off. And that was a look that represented my brand and what I stood for at the time. At the end of the 60-minute appointment, the guy I was meeting actually hugged me with gratitude and booked four more sessions on the spot. That day when I added him on Twitter, I was his eighth follower. The last time I checked he had 89,000!

This is such an important point – possibly the most important point of all. This guy saw the true value in meeting with me (possibly before I even understood the true value I could offer myself). He didn't see AU$500 as an indulgence but instead an investment in his future and I hope, and he has since told me, that meeting with me those few times and exchanging a fee for my experience and intellectual property saved him far more by avoiding failures and mistakes that could have cost his fragile, first-stage start-up hundreds of thousands of dollars.

That's not to say everyone was willing to pay and, of course, some people were totally put off by a price tag, either because they genuinely couldn't afford it or because they had the money but weren't open to investing in themselves. But I learned not to take a "no" personally, and there was no shortage of people who said "yes". At one point, we were averaging five meetings a week, which meant an additional AU$2500 per week, AU$10,000 a month, more than AU$120,000 a year over and above our core revenue streams.

But it wasn't really about the money (it never is for me). Most importantly, it marked a huge psychological shift for me. I no longer begrudgingly met with people, I was able to give even more of myself in these meetings, I found that my ideas were flowing and my energy was off the Richter scale. My clients were certainly getting their money's worth and I was being remunerated. It was a win-win for both of us. Kerching!

It does not matter how slowly you

go as long as you do not stop

-Confucius

WOULD YOU BURN A $5 NOTE?

The most simple and powerful piece of advice I can give to anyone, whether you're an entrepreneur, freelancer, office worker or somewhere in between, is to not only know your day rate and your hourly rate but also your five-minute rate. Yes, how much is five minutes of your time, skill set, conversation or brain worth? There are many online tools that can help you calculate this if you search on Google, and it's well worth taking a few moments to do it.

It might sound pernickety, but just think of all these five-minute sections as $5 bills. Would you just toss them out of your car window as you were driving? No! Because you realise that all those $5 bills could add up to a fortune over a lifetime.

Knowing your five-minute rate will help you make logical scheduling decisions – should you hire a personal assistant or do your admin yourself, is the cost of getting a taxi to that meeting justifiable because you'll get there faster, should you travel across the city to meet that person for a coffee or politely say you can't make it? If you know the true value of your time, you can assess, calculate and evaluate fairly.

On the wall in my office I have a quote from the American poet Ralph Waldo Emerson who said, "Guard well your spare moments. They are like uncut diamonds. Discard them and their value will never be known. Improve them and they will become the brightest gems in a useful life." So, what is five minutes of your time worth to you? And what is five minutes of your time worth to others?

It's always useful when thinking about time and money to talk in cold, hard figures. Take away your ego or your modesty and really think practically. I recently discovered an amazing online tool called Meeting Ticker, which allows you to calculate how much money is spent attending a meeting. The idea is that at the start of a meeting you log onto the website, input the number of attendees, your average hourly rate, then press 'Start' when the meeting officially begins. On your computer screen throughout the meeting, a counter flashes up calculating the rising cost of the manpower involved. If there are four executives in a meeting, a 60-minute session could add up to thousands, which is sobering if you've spent half the time discussing the weather or Kim Kardashian's latest magazine cover.

Let's look at this like a mathematician. How many hours are there in a day, and how effectively are you using them? I remember meeting an amazingly ambitious woman at an event recently, who had a full-time job working in environmental conservation, but also in her free time volunteered for various charities and taught yoga. High-achiever alert! One day her mentor asked her to do an exercise where she wrote down all of her projects and how many hours they took to complete, including preparation time around them. A yoga class might only be 60 minutes long but then there's the travel time and how long it takes to plan classes. "I added up all the hours and I was pleasantly surprised," she told me, "I still had two and a half hours free in each day. I thought I'd be far busier." Then she realised she hadn't factored in any time for sleep. Or eating. Those two and a half hours were the only personal time she had left after her external commitments.

So, you see how all those extra five-minute segments can quickly add up and emotionally bankrupt you, and why it's important to examine and break down what time is worth to you.

Although she was paid AU$40 for an hour yoga class, it also took 90 minutes to travel there and 60 minutes to prepare, which meant she was paid AU$40 for three and a half hours, at an hourly rate of just over AU$11. Not to mention the fact she was sleep-deprived and her relationship with her partner was suffering.

This is why I now schedule blocks of 'nothing' into my email calendar. Really. If you saw my calendar you'd notice lavender-coloured 10- or 15-minute blocks dotted between my meetings, events and speaking gigs that are just as vital to my productivity as anything else on my to-do list, because they mean it's time for me to stop, breathe, reboot, rehydrate, grab a snack, go to the toilet or just sit and stare into space. It's amazing how in a frantic week these basic human needs can be forgotten. It might seem crazy having to formally schedule in nothing, but it's all part of my process for valuing my own time, my own needs and my own boundaries.

You may not be in a position to charge $500 an hour or $10,000 a day (I wasn't always, believe me) but nobody's time is worth zero and every cent of your personal currency matters. The phrase "time is money" might sound like a line from a cheesy movie, but it is pretty appropriate, and I think more of us need to remember it. How valuable is your time, and how do you really want to spend it? I'm certainly not saying you should cancel every coffee meeting and lock yourself in a sound-proof box so you can focus, focus, focus without any interruptions. I'm also not saying you must always opt for the most profitable use of your time, but just be aware of the facts and figures so you can make informed choices.

Sometimes I walk for an hour to meet a university student who's asked me for help on a business project, I might skip work to spend the day with a friend who's just broken up with her boyfriend, often I leave the office in the middle of the afternoon for 15 minutes just to lay in the park and ground myself. But I make all these decisions knowing quite analytically and mathematically at a gut level, after years of trial and tribulation, exactly how much my time is worth and the emotional, financial and professional trade-off if I choose to give it to others without a financial exchange.

On the wall of my office, which is covered in a tapestry of touch points to inspire me, I also have a quote from the American poet Carl Sandburg who said, "Time is the coin of your life. It is the only coin you have, and only you can determine how it will be spent. Be careful lest you let other people spend it for you."

If you are not willing to risk the unusual, you will have to settle for The ordinary. —Jim Rohn

4 WAYS TO WORK LESS AND EARN MORE

OUTSOURCE

I've had a cleaner since way before I could afford a cleaner. But in my early twenties, someone wise once pointed out that I could either pay someone who was actually good at the task to top-to-toe my flat in an hour, or I could waste an entire morning bumbling around trying to do it myself, when really my time would be better spent putting my own skill set (networking, negotiating, visioning) to good use. I'm a big believer in outsourcing your weaknesses, whether that's getting a personal trainer to ensure you hit your exercise goals (remember health is the #1 priority) or getting a virtual PA to spreadsheet your expenses. I pretty much outsource anything I can these days.

ADD A FIFTH

I read an article by Forbes financial reporter Kathy Caprino, where she recommends that entrepreneurs who suspect they're undercharging clients should add 20 per cent to their fees – right now. "Then figure out what the right number is within the next few months, and start charging it," writes Kathy. There really is no better time to make changes than right now, before another day, week, month, year has passed and another $100, $1000, $10,000 is missed. It does take courage but if I hadn't done it, I have no doubt my business wouldn't be around today.

CUT YOUR E-OUTPUT

We all know emails can be a time zap. According to the 2014-2018 Email Statistics Report, the average worker receives 121 emails each day. That's the equivalent of reading a mid-sized novel every week. The question is, how many of those words were simply unnecessary, either because the writers were repeating themselves, overemphasising a point or filling space with social etiquette? Let's all agree to a bit of brevity in e-correspondence and get to the point quicker. It's not bad manners, it's business sense.

DON'T SWEAT THE SMALL STUFF

I have an entrepreneurial friend who says sometimes his worries virtually paralyse him – he gets so overwhelmed by the 'what-ifs' that rather than tackling them he literally sits at his computer staring at the screen, unable to move because he feels so bogged down in what to tackle first. As an entrepreneur you will have to put out fires – daily – and it is a time zap, especially if you allow it to overwhelm you. So, I have a few tricks to reboot my mind and get ready for action, whether it's a quick five-minute dance party in my office, a walk around the block or reading a chapter of an inspirational book. It's like a 'control, alt, delete' function for my psyche.

HOW TO MASTER YOUR MARK-UPS

A mark-up is defined as the difference between what a retailer will pay for a product and its retail price paid by the customer. When setting a price for a product it can be difficult to know where to set your benchmark – too high and you'll drive away customers, too low and you'll burn out your business before you've even started. The key to calculating the mark-up to put on a product is research, starting with the combined fixed and variable outgoings your company will face in the next year of business.

If you are making a physical product, then start by getting quotes from suppliers for raw materials. This can be where many start-ups underestimate because many suppliers will offer a special rate to win new customers. Don't let your estimations be swayed by a one-off discount that has an expiry date. If you're offering a service that isn't tangible, then calculate the number of hours it will take to complete a task and the cost per hour, as well as any additional fees such as, in the case of building a website, the purchasing of stock images or fonts.

Another factor is how much your competitors are charging, because this will determine whether you can make a splash in the market. But never simply match their price, as remember that you don't know the ins and outs of their overheads – they may have a special deal on rent or long-term mates rates from a supplier. It's important that your margins cover your overheads. Use their figure as a comparison but don't simply clone it. Look at your own, individual situation so you can make an objective decision.

Many retailers still use the 'keystone' mark-up model as a starting point. This means doubling the cost of the wholesale or production cost of your product (remember to factor in shipping and packaging costs as well). Many entrepreneurs think it's better to aim slightly higher than to undercharge, because if you realise later you've incorrectly priced your product or service, customers will be more welcoming of a price drop than a price hike (in fact, they'll be rejoicing). At the end of the day, setting a margin is really down to 'value-based' pricing. How much value does a customer attach to the impact your unique offering can make to their life?

Chapter 4

Systems + Strategies

ess than 18 months after the launch of *The Collective* I lost AU$61,000. I don't mean I 'lost' it in the sense that I struck a bad business deal and made a loss. I mean I physically lost it, misplaced it, forgot about it, as if it were a $5 note that I'd stuffed in an old coat pocket, not a sizeable sum that could make or break my start-up. Okay, I'll explain – this was a few months after we launched our Collective Hub website, the next platform for the business. Money was tight. How tight? Use tea bags twice tight. I kept staring at my profit and loss statements, receivables, payables etc. with this niggling feeling that I had forgotten something, and this went on and on for weeks!

Then one day a member of the web team walked past my office on the way to the kitchen holding a china mug that, quite aptly, had the slogan "I'm with stupid" printed on the side. And I realised she was – with stupid, that is. I had completely and utterly forgotten the entire revenue stream from the website, months' worth of payments received by the recently added online store that were going into a separate account. We had designed it that way on purpose, but in the midst of the bustling, ever-evolving, every-day-there-is-something-new activity of the office, I'd forgotten all about it. And it's not like I was rolling in money at the time; this was the equivalent of going out of the house with just your pants on and not your top.

Why am I telling you this slightly embarrassing story, when I know it just serves to amplify my acute lack of attention to detail? Because it's perfect proof of the importance of systems and strategies, and how they can make you or break you if they are perfectly in line or the absolute opposite. As you may have noticed, because it's a theme that underplays all of my books, I have a slightly holistic approach to business, relying on gut instinct, intuition, passion, will power, visualisation and manifestation to spur me on, guide my decisions and draw people to me. BUT (and it's a big 'but'), when it comes to money we have to be a little pragmatic, practical and rational. We have to put in place systems, processes, strategies and people that will support us, report to us, monitor us and keep us in check. It might sound ridiculous that I 'lost' AU\$61,000, especially at a point in my business when literally every single last dollar and cent was paramount, but it can be that easy to lose track with poor systems, and this is how many good businesses go under.

The truth is that sometimes as an entrepreneur you can't make clear decisions. As much as we all like to pretend we're superheroes who are 100 per cent 'on' all of the time, there are days, weeks, even months, when for myriad reasons – maybe you're rundown, maybe your parent is sick, or your children are acting up or other people's naysaying starts to get you down – you can't see things clearly, your vision gets blurred and you can't assess your business realistically. I call it wearing "fear goggles" and we've all been there at some point, whether it's in our love life, work or even a hobby, and we're convinced that we're failing, we're useless, it's over. Even if, in actual fact, we're perfectly okay.

Do you have a clear idea of how much money you have, can earn and owe? Really? I have an entrepreneurial friend who calls it "business dysmorphic disorder" – when you can't stop thinking about a flaw in your business – a flaw that is either minor, imagined or exaggerated. But to you, your business seems so disastrous that you can't see how you can continue. This is where we need systems and strategies to check ourselves, analyse ourselves, protect ourselves (I'll cover this more in chapter eight) and make a clear decision about how to take action and just how drastic our situation is. Although business is a game, so is chess, and yet some experts make that an art form because they study it, strategise it and practise it relentlessly. I have to agree with Tony Hsieh, the founder of Zappos, who says, "Don't play games that you don't understand – even if you see other people making money from them."

GET YOUR GEEK ON

I recently read an interview with Derek Flanzraich, the founder of health and wellness site Greatist, who says, "So much of entrepreneurship is future-focused. Especially in terms of funding and revenue generation – it's tough sometimes to remember you need enough money in the bank today." I couldn't agree more, although I certainly haven't always got this right in the past. But then, as you know, I'm always happy to learn from my mistakes (no matter how silly they can make me look).

I am the first to admit that I have, in the past, and sometimes (okay, often) still in the present, suffered because of an appalling lack of attention to detail. What can I say? I am a big-picture thinker, a universal dreamer, always scanning the far-reaching horizon, absorbed in the beauty of the landscape rather than counting the trees and the sheep in the paddocks. But I've learned over 14 years in my own business that I have to force myself to crunch numbers. Constantly.

And it's a good thing that I've discovered my inner geek at this time, because when you have a global business with multiple touch points, distributors, projects, side products and production points, that is a LOT of data to work through. The weirdest thing is, to my amazement, I now find myself actually enjoying crunching numbers. What started out as a chore is now kind of satisfying, and I get a sense of pride in knowing every teeny tiny decimal point, in seeing not only the bigger revenue streams, but also the smaller estuaries and the tiniest raindrops. And I'm thankful for it – for years I ran a small, one-dimensional business.

You might be thinking, "but you 'only' run a magazine". However, the magazine is just one component of the business and within it are layers and layers of data that all need to be compared against each other. This is what a lot of entrepreneurs have to remember. It's not just a case of how the current issue of the print magazine is selling. That's just the tip of the iceberg. How is *The Collective* selling in newsagents versus subscriptions, in WHSmith versus NewsLink, on iSUBSCRiBE versus Magshop? How is the print magazine selling versus the digital versions on PressReader versus Zinio versus Magshop? How is the website doing versus the print magazine? How is Tuesday's EDM comparing to Thursday's EDM? How is *Life & Love* selling versus *Daring & Disruptive*, how are they selling in physical stores versus on online stores, in Norway compared to Switzerland, in newsagents, airports, through our online store, on Booktopia and Amazon, how are the e-books doing compared to the print versions – and what are the margins on all of the above? I could go on and on… And sometimes I do!

There is so much data to analyse in business every single day, no matter its size. It blows my mind sometimes, and yet every morning without fail I force myself to sit down and check through the figures, so that I can make clear, logical, sensible, pragmatic decisions – all without my 'fear goggles' on. It means that when a staff member comes to me and asks if she can fly interstate for a conference, I can be objective rather than reactive. I can stand back and look at the stats. Okay, it's going to cost x, but what are the potential returns, the creativity/innovation/ education investment or the cultural knock-on effects to the rest of the team? If every staff member went to a conference this month, would it be financially viable, beneficial or practical? While we want to promote a flowing, freeing, encouraging culture, I am still all about the numbers… numbers, numbers, numbers. That is because I have to be. And trust me – I was NEVER wired this way, but I think at the bottom of it all, I always wanted to have it exactly like this and much, much bigger.

The problem with many start-ups, I believe, comes when the founder has a surface view of its data and doesn't take the time to delve and probe – perhaps because they've never been shown how to. A 2014 Intuit study of 500 small business owners in Canada found that 44 per cent had below-basic financial literacy skills. Perhaps it's no surprise then that, according to Statistics Canada data, only 50 per cent of start-ups in that country survive to their fifth anniversary. (On a passing positive note, the number of start-ups now surviving past four years in Australia is roughly 50 per cent.)

Do you have a bit of a mental block when it comes to data? Have you convinced yourself it's out of your skill set, just because you didn't get an A in maths class and can't remember how to do long division? It's time to get out of that self-sabotaging, financially toxic mindset, because if I can do it (and yes, I failed maths too) then you certainly can. I always say that a lot of my business decisions are 90 per cent gut instinct. However, I believe that my gut feeling is so finely tuned, connected and switched on because I also do the legwork to understand my business, my market, my industry and the outside factors that can have an impact. Just think of all these facts, figures and analyses as the probiotics to my gut instinct, supporting, protecting and honing it.

The good news is that as a modern entrepreneur, it's easier to keep track of data than ever before thanks to data-for-dummies technology that can allow any of us to number crunch like experts. Although that doesn't mean it should make experts redundant, as I'll touch on in a moment, it does mean we can all boost our financial literacy, so that when it comes to our own businesses, we're not the equivalent of a kid at a fair trying to count how many lollies there are in a jar.

Okay, so what are my recommendations? Embrace innovation and find accounting software that will give you everything you need when you need it, and in a way that you can digest. This has been so helpful to me as someone who, early on, had absolutely no idea what was happening in our finances. Once I could see it, I could make informed, strategic decisions. Without it, it's just a guessing game.

I was chatting to a tech entrepreneur at an event recently who admitted he loves any software that comes with a smartphone app, because it means he can do his financial homework during random down-moments, when he's waiting for an elevator or sitting on the toilet (I do love strangers who overshare as much as I do!). We're living in a world where there really is no excuse for not keeping abreast of every financial breath, cough and hiccup of your business, you just need to arm yourself with the systems and strategies to make it easy... well, maybe not easy, but doable and weirdly enjoyable. I swear that it really is quite addictive once those numbers stop being a blur and those cents start to make sense again.

There are many options available and as we go to print, I don't doubt new competitors are appearing, and each has different elements that suit different types of businesses, freelancers, entrepreneurs or anyone trying to get a handle of their finances. We use Xero but there's MYOB, Reckon, QuickBooks Online, Cheqbook, Kashoo, Wave and Zoho Books, and the list goes on. Founded in New Zealand, Xero describes itself as "beautiful accountancy software". Bet you never thought you'd call a spreadsheet beautiful, right? But it kind of is! I recently attended a tech event with Ashton Kutcher (shameless name drop) who said, "We need to remember that smart is sexy", and so is money management. Stop rolling your eyes, it really can be!

The reason we opted for Xero is that it gives us a real-time update of cash flow. Everything is synced – the invoices you send, the expenses you file, your staff payroll, your purchase orders and any ingoings and outgoings from your bank account. It's like a Facebook feed for your finances. It's even won over the traditional accounting community, and I know tons of accountants who recommend it to their clients (well, it makes their job easier too).

Don't expect more than
you need to be happy

— but definitely
don't accept less!

BANK ON OTHER PEOPLE

There is no 'I' in profit. Well, okay there is, but there really shouldn't be! Show me a millionaire who claims to have made their fortune entirely on their own and I will show you a humongous fibber. The reality is, to build a successful business you need a trusted team of advisors and experts when it comes to money – an accountant, bank manager, lawyer, CFO, bookkeeper. You might not need all of these pillars, but you'll certainly need some of them to help build your business, bolster it, support it and add structure in chaos.

I recently read a blog on LinkedIn called 'Owner/CEO: Who holds you accountable? God? Bank manager?', which argues that businesses fail when "no one but your gremlins keeps you true and accountable for your behaviour and results." There is a lot of truth in this and it's why, despite being the only founder and investor in my business, I am the first to say that I don't do it alone. I put people in place to support me (and check up on me). As I bang on about – a lot! – I'm a big believer in hiring to your weaknesses, particularly when it comes to finances.

There is no shame in saying you need help, whether you're an entrepreneur who needs an accountant, a mother who has a nanny or a celebrity who spends three hours with a make-up artist before a premiere. When it comes to running a profitable business, let's stop presenting the image of, "I woke up like this" and admit that it actually takes a lot of hard work, a bagful of tools, an expert's guidance and half an inch of foundation to gloss over the cracks each day.

Two years before the launch of *The Collective* I wrote a book about property investing, which became one of the most successful books I've ever published. I only wrote it because so many people kept asking me how I did it – how did I have a portfolio of houses when I appeared to funnel all my spare cash into my business? Sometimes I wondered how I did it myself. I had a chunk of cash to start with, but I made good buying decisions – I purchased houses for under the market value, so when they were re-evaluated by the banks, I had a lot of equity at my disposal to buy the next one. But this happened because I had the right people in my camp helping me make great decisions at every turn. I wrote a book dedicated to it and the 'dream team' who helped me – my mortgage broker, my bank manager, my trusty estate agent. They are the ones who really made my property portfolio possible.

To a degree, it's the same when you're running a business. Oh, you might not need the whole arsenal of advisors and experts just yet, but I recommend you consider recruiting at least a few from the A-team in the section below, where I have listed their roles, responsibilities and benefits, so you can see which apply best to you.

Just like any partnership, relationship or collaboration, you need to find experts who are compatible with you, your personality, your ethics, your morals and your end vision. In *Daring & Disruptive* I wrote about how I had to temporarily "break-up" with my accountant when we first launched *The Collective* because he thought I was taking too much of a risk (although we've since reunited). Think of it this way: if one hairdresser doesn't want to dye your hair pink because they think it's too raucous, would you listen to them and dye it brown? I hope not! I would tell you to walk out the door, walk down the street and go into the salon with the skull and crossbones painted on the window and see what they say.

I ask one thing from all my team, whether they're in-house staff members, freelancers or my financial support team – please believe in me 100 per cent or, thanks but no thanks, let's go our separate ways. It is so important to find experts that trust your intuition as much as you do because the truth is (and I know I'm going to contradict myself here after going on about the importance of data), there are times when you will still make decisions based purely on gut instinct. I do it.

Every. Single. Day. I'm 90 per cent wired this way but only because I've got 14-plus years of runs on the board and a team to support me and keep me in check.

A classic quote by William Bruce Cameron says, "Not everything that can be counted counts, and not everything that counts can be counted." This is something I remind my accountant of when I make a decision that doesn't look sensible on paper. As a serial entrepreneur, I don't always need to look at spreadsheets to gauge a situation. After producing so many issues of *The Collective* (I still pinch myself every time we go to print!), I can tell within 20 minutes of posting a photo of our latest cover on social media if that issue of the magazine is going to sell a moderate amount or break our records, from the reaction of gen-public. It's the same sense that tells me, within an employee's first week, if she or he is going to be with us for the long haul, and allows me to smell a business opportunity, even if there is a level of risk attached to it and everyone else is shying away. The experts I surround myself with somehow know when to push me, when to stop me, when to question me, when to encourage me, and allow me to see my bottom line not as a concrete floor but as a trampoline that I can jump on to reach amazing heights.

There is no exercise better
for the heart than reaching
down and lifting people up.

—John A Holmes

THE ENTREPRENEUR'S A-TEAM

ACCOUNTANT

WHAT THEY SHOULD DO: The numbers guy or girl. There to prepare financial statements, including balance sheets and analysis of financial records, cash flow strategies and – most importantly – handle tax return preparation.

WHAT YOU SHOULD ASK: "What do you see in the future?" A good accountant will have one foot in the present and one foot in the future, specifically five years from now, able to put processes in place that can grow with you and achieve your goals for that period.

WHERE TO FIND THEM: From my experience, ask for referrals from like-minded entrepreneurs who have a similar approach to growth, cash flow and risk that you do. As I've said in the pages of this book, I once had to part ways with mine because we simply weren't on the same page. If you feel the same way, ask around and don't be afraid to jump ship – there will be one out there to help you navigate your unique financial journey.

BOOKKEEPER

WHAT THEY SHOULD DO: Often seen as the cheaper, younger cousin of your accountant. Bookkeepers are professionals who specialise in tasks around keeping track of cash flow, invoicing, some budgeting and expenditure analysis and date entry of the aforementioned, but they don't have the same formal qualifications as accountants do.

WHAT YOU SHOULD ASK: "Can you sign a confidentiality agreement?" Bookkeepers aren't bound by the same code of conduct as accountants in many countries, but they will be privy to all your private information, so it's wise to put a contract in place to ensure that loose lips don't sink ships.

WHERE TO FIND THEM: Word of mouth recommendations are again a good starting point. I feel like my bookkeeper is an extension of my family because we communicate so often and about really important issues in the business' life, so it's important that they not only have the right skills to navigate the often tricky financial journey of a start-up, but that they also have the right personality and temperament to fit with yours.

This role has been crucial to the success of my own business journey to date, and in my experience you get what you pay for.

CHIEF FINANCIAL OFFICER (CFO)

WHAT THEY SHOULD DO: More than just a head for figures, a good CFO acts as a trusted advisor to the CEO of a company, on all matters from fundraising to deal-making, lucrative partnerships, international growth and hiring and firing.

WHAT YOU SHOULD ASK: "Can you multi-task?" The role of a CFO, especially in a start-up, is multi-layered. While the role used to be more about balance sheets, the responsibilities are now far broader, focusing on the best ways to model and scale a business (as Forbes puts it, they are no longer "bean counters" but instead are "bean sprouters"). This can include everything from new product development to social media presence.

WHERE TO FIND THEM: LinkedIn is a good place to start searching, as – like it or not – finding a savvy CFO could require some poaching. Check out the CFOs of start-ups you admire and see if they're open to new opportunities. If they're not, they may be able to recommend someone else equally talented.

VIRTUAL ASSISTANT (VA)

WHAT THEY SHOULD DO: Be the bridge between a bookkeeper or accountant when you can't afford them. Ideal for a solo-preneur or a bedroom business with a small turnover, a virtual assistant can be an admin angel, performing tasks such as inputting expenses into spreadsheets, chasing invoices and doing research into the cost of upcoming overheads.

WHAT YOU SHOULD ASK: "How much do you charge per hour?" Most virtual assistants charge by the job or by the hour, so alway ask for an estimation.

WHERE TO FIND THEM: If you're on social media, post a shout-out saying you're looking for one as VAs are notoriously active on social media and eager to secure new business. Don't narrow your search down to VAs in your neighbourhood, because it's normal for a business to work with a VA in a totally different country.

SOUNDING BOARD

WHAT THEY SHOULD DO: Listen, and from time to time offer wise counsel.

WHAT YOU SHOULD ASK: Rhetorical questions. Let's face it, after a bad day you've gone to this friend or family member for a rant because they're a soothing shoulder to cry on, not because they actually have any financial experience. Their main role is to pass the tissues.

WHERE TO FIND THEM: Not at a networking event. The best sounding boards are mates who aren't at all involved in your industry, and so can remind you that it doesn't really matter if a client takes three days longer to pay an invoice and that the sky won't fall in if your competitor launches their website before you do.

A MENTOR OR ADVISER

WHAT THEY SHOULD DO: Tell you how it is.

WHAT YOU SHOULD ASK: "Can we fight and still be friends?" Because there will be times when you will disagree and so you should, seeing you're a disruptor, but there is nothing better than having a wiser, been-there-before (or at least been-somewhere-similar) person to chat with.

WHERE TO FIND THEM: Over time, carefully handpick them based on watching their success, failure and how they have responded to both.

LAWYER

WHAT THEY SHOULD DO: Help you before you get into trouble, and especially if you do. Lawyers can be expensive but I've also learned the hard way that they are crucial in any business journey and it's helpful to be on the front foot with everything big or small, from domain name ownership to employment contracts.

WHAT YOU SHOULD ASK: "What do you specialise in?" We have different lawyers for all manner of things... intellectual property, defamation, copyright etc.

WHERE TO FIND THEM: Networking events, colleague recommendations, even lawyers themselves as they will point you to those who specialise in something they don't.

HOW TO GET PAST A GATEKEEPER

I am in the lucky position that in 14 years of working for myself, I have never had to borrow a single cent from a bank. This isn't to say I've never had dealings with them, and people like them. I have had to convince a lot of very conventional penny-pushers in roles tied up in red tape and bureaucracy to take a punt on my vision, even though I probably seemed like a huge risk.

In *Daring & Disruptive* I wrote about the terrifying meeting I had during the birth of *The Collective* with one of Australia's biggest banks, where I had to pitch my big vision and why I believed it was profitable. Just to clarify, this wasn't a pitch for a bank loan but a sponsorship deal, where I offered the bank in question advertising pages, syndicated content and branded speaking gigs, in exchange for a cash injection that I didn't need to ever pay back.

Because of this 'back-door approach', rather than meeting with a member of the investment team, I sat down with the head of their marketing department. This might sound less intimidating, but really does little to increase your chances of getting a 'yes', as all business proposals of any kind really need to meet the same strict, stringent criteria. Does she have a proven track record? Does she have valid experience? How big a risk is her proposition? Is there a market? Will it meet our objectives? Etc.

People always ask me how I get people to say "yes!" Many people I've spoken to complain of emailing or phoning people and never hearing back. My first questions are always – how long ago did you contact them, how many times, are you being impatient? In the ideal world, it would take one email to get someone's attention but sometimes it's about chinking away at their armour. For example, if I want to get in front of the marketing director of a major company, I will read absolutely everything about them (it helps to set up a Google alert for their name) and then every single time they get a win I'll send them an email, if they get a new position I'll send them a hand-written congratulations card, when I bring out a new book I'll send them a signed copy. It might take a year to get on their radar but for the cost of a few cards or bunches of flowers, you might end up with a deal worth hundreds of thousands.

Another approach I use is playing to their ego – because we all have one – and to their more humane side. Don't go in pleading, "Can you help me?" Instead, suggest a way that you can help them. Years ago, a recruitment company approached me and asked for my help getting the attention of HR directors in a number of big corporations, who at that point weren't returning their calls. I said they didn't stand a chance… unless they had a back-door strategy. "Why don't you write a book about the best way to get hired by a big business?"

I suggested. "Call those HR directors and say you're looking for experts to offer quotes on the topic." You might call it an underhand tactic, but suddenly the same HR directors wanted to meet them, the book was published and the recruitment company had a full black book of contacts to pitch their business to. A friend admitted that when she was buying her last property, she just happened to "mention" to the estate agent she was speaking to that she was writing an article on how to buy-to-let and needed experts to quote in the piece. The article did get published, the estate agents she mentioned got publicity, and she got the best customer service of her life.

Whatever your back-door strategy, there's always a right and wrong way to do it, as the entrepreneur I know who tried to win over a bank manager by first dating his daughter will testify. No, it didn't end well. Okay, so you've got a meeting, you're sitting on the other side of the desk from the head honcho who holds the purse strings. Now, how do you impress them, excite them and intrigue them? If you google 'business proposal' there are hundreds and thousands of websites offering ready-made templates for pitches. But I don't think many disruptive start-ups fit particularly well into a standard business plan. And so it's time to think outside the box, have faith in yourself and hope they follow suit.

A few weeks before writing this, in the lead up to *The Collective's* second birthday, I had a meeting with one of the biggest supermarkets in the world, who at this point didn't stock *The Collective* because they hadn't done a review of their titles in two years, which means they hadn't taken on any new titles since before we existed. However, I'd heard that a new guy had started in a role in that division and so, after sending him a "congrats" card (touch points, touch points) he agreed to meet me. The problem is, straight away he admitted that his hands were still tied and he'd been told by his new bosses not to take on any new publications for at least another year. Did I shake his hand and leave? No! I told him to take a proposition to his bosses. If he stocked us I would guarantee profit. Guarantee it! His eyebrows shot up. "I've never heard anyone say that

It's a
beautiful
life ...
live it on purpose,
with passion
and tenacity,
but above all,
with grace
and dignity.

before," he admitted. I don't doubt that. I know some entrepreneurs reading this would be thinking I'm mad making such a statement, but I knew this idea was a winning one (I've had enough ideas to know which will have traction) and am willing to back myself. So he took the proposition to his bosses, and the rest is history…

My point to all this is that I believe many disruptive entrepreneurs can make the mistake of falling into an 'us and them' mentality and seeing traditional corporations, financial institutions or those within organisations who count the pennies as, if not enemies, then certainly not their allies. But just because someone works within a global conglomerate, it doesn't mean they don't have a disruptive vision. Just because they have traditional protocol to follow, it doesn't mean there isn't a loophole. And if you have really exhausted all traditional avenues, don't despair, as there are always many more fundraising or support-soliciting options, which I'll go into later.

The most important points to remember are to know your value, make them an offer they've never heard before and, above all, remember that you're also doing them a favour by allowing them to come on your journey with you. You might never get your collaborator to dance around the office with you (although I'll continue to try) but your start-up's victories should at least make them do a little jig inside.

The Seven Social Sins
according to Mahatma Gandhi

1. Politics without principles
2. Wealth without work
3. Pleasure without conscience
4. Knowledge without character
5. Commerce without morality
6. Science without humanity
7 Worship without sacrifice

Chapter 5

Money for Nothing

As anyone who has read *Daring & Disruptive* knows, I am not a fan of investing in time-zapping, expensive prototypes or the kind of complex business plans that make *War and Peace* seem like a quick read. Not at first anyway, not until you know for certain an idea has legs and is worth investing in financially and emotionally. This is where the practice of making money from nothing comes in – and by 'nothing', I mean just an idea.

In this instance, I had enough faith in myself, my conversational skills and my ability to paint a picture with my words to know I didn't need a visual prop. I'm not saying that I could guarantee 100 per cent they would say 'yes' to it, but if I did get a 'no' it wouldn't be because I hadn't sold it well enough. Sometimes rejection comes for a multitude of reasons – bad timing, bad moods, bad business sense – then be doubly thankful you haven't wasted time and money trying to convince them. I come from the 'fail fast' school of entrepreneurs. I am at peace with the idea that not every idea works, but I do want to lose as little – financially and emotionally – in that loss as possible.

This means getting an idea in front of the people that matter (whether it's possible partners, distributors or customers) quickly – the day, the hour after an idea is first brainstormed – to gauge their reaction. Who has time to create a complex mock-up? And even if you do, you often end up talking to the document rather than from your heart, which is where the secret lies. You can always provide people with well-thought-out documents after a meeting if they were captured by your concept. I am famous for going into meetings with just a page of notes or one diagram (I call it "vapourware").

Of course, selling an idea without a prop is a brave approach that takes a humungous amount of faith in yourself. It's like the equivalent of going on a first date without make-up, you have to trust that your recipient will see the potential in the rawness and share your vision of the future. But in the case of *The Collective*, where we are constantly brainstorming, pitching, growing, expanding, collaborating and making deals, being able to sell nothing is a substantial saver. Just do the maths – if an idea takes four hours of manpower to mockup, with two ideas a week, that's 416 hours a year.

In the Internet age it's more important than ever to be able to win people over without anything concrete. It was in 1937 that marketing expert Elmer Wheeler coined the phrase "Don't sell the steak. Sell the sizzle." That's exactly what I did when looking for sponsorship for *The Collective*. It's what I've always done. I wasn't selling a one-off product – a bunch of words and pictures printed on paper. I was selling a feeling – a sense of belonging, an inspiring, uplifting community that made you feel part of something. I was armed with nothing but my passion. And that connects, like really connects with people. It might sound a bit woo-woo but it did pay off and continues to.

Just like anything, the ability to make money from nothing is a skill that can be honed and practised. My top tip for this is to BE EXCITED. Yes, the kind of excited that needs CAPITAL LETTERS! In early 2015 I was lucky enough to be invited to a talk with Ashton Kutcher (there I go again) when he came to Australia with the technology company Lenovo that he works with as a product developer. He spoke about the best piece of advice that he and his famous friends had ever been given, and one piece of advice – from Taylor Swift no less – really stuck with me. "Enthusiasm can protect you from absolutely anything." It's true, enthusiasm can fill a gap in knowledge, a gap in experience, and if you're REALLY, REALLY EXCITED – I don't mean fake it, I mean genuinely – other people will be swept up in your vision. Mock-up or no mock-up.

An awesome example of this strategy at work comes from Greg Gianforte, the co-founder of cloud-based software company RightNow Technologies, whose first product was a program that helped companies reply to clients' emails. It was a product he took to market before it even existed. In 1997, after seeing a gap in the market, he boldly started cold-calling customer support managers at hundreds of companies, to tell them such software would be available in 90 days and ask if they were interested. If they said no he asked why, and so killed two birds with one stone. He not only found customers but also did market research that helped develop his product.

It was a high-risk strategy, as what if the product hadn't been possible to make? Fast-forward to October 2011, and Oracle Corporation announced it had agreed to buy RightNow Technologies for US$1.5 billion. The good news is this strategy is really available to anyone, and let's remember that Greg wasn't being a fraudster, in fact, he gave away the software for free in many cases in the beginning to create some buzz in the market.

I'm in the interesting situation, now that that the business and myself have enjoyed a bit of success, that I spend all day every day not only pitching to other people, but also being pitched to. And so I can say from experience that if you come to me with a 50-page business plan printed on shiny paper, with colourful pie charts, graphics and glossy photographs, it means nothing to me if I don't see a sparkle in your eye when you're explaining it.

Likewise, I've said yes to pitches where that person has, quite literally, walked into my office empty-handed, because I can see their heart is full of passion (and they are clearly clever and are connected with like-minded people). I also once, memorably, agreed to a sponsorship proposal from a highly enthusiastic marketing manager who had a brainwave on the bus to my office and wrote his idea on his arm in biro. I'm not kidding!

Now, I'm not saying there is no place for complex research, exploration, spreadsheets, diagrams and mind maps, but don't do this too prematurely. Wait until you at least know there's a hint of market desire. I am a pro-prototype, but not pre-pitch type of person. Are you with me? If not, I can draw you a diagram on a napkin...

PROMISES, PROMISES...

Even from the very start of *The Collective* I never wanted to shrink. I had a big voice but a small budget, and so I had to find back-door solutions to financial problems. I knew early on when I decided to take the consumer market route as opposed to just B2B that I wanted the magazine to be placed in newsstands at airports because, as we all know, airport travellers are big magazine and book buyers. Even people who rarely buy magazines are often tempted to at a departure gate. But I didn't just want to be on the shelf among all our comrades (I don't like the word "competitors" as I think we have a unique product and I'm a big believer in reciprocity and abundance and that there is enough room for everyone). I decided I also wanted floor-to-ceiling light walls. You know the light-up billboards on the shop front of newsagents? Unfortunately, these prime marketing positions do not come cheap. It costs thousands upon thousands. Which you have to pay up-front.

It was completely cost-prohibitive, so even if I wanted to I didn't have that kind of money to fund such a bold marketing move. But I knew I had to come out of the blocks big or it would be a very slow burn. So, I sold them a proposition – can you take the product, sell it and then take the money for the light walls from your profit? It was a huge risk! Remember at this point we hadn't even brought out one issue of the magazine. We had no evidence that anyone would buy it, let alone that newsagents stocking it would make a profit. Or riskier still, I would make no money and have no way to pay them. But this is one of those moments when gut feeling drove my business decision. I had to back myself and believe in myself… and now you'll see not only *The Collective* magazine splashed across airport light walls, but also campaigns for all my books (and yes I did take an excited photograph next to one when I flew to the Gold Coast recently – but wouldn't you?).

I have done these types of deals over and over and over again with
The Collective, all over the world. Just eight months after the magazine launched
I flew to Toronto with my marketing director. We had two days of back-to-back
meetings with distributors who had converged on the city for a global media
distributors conference. It was a big expense, and for my level of experience at the
time I was a little out of my depth (but I didn't tell them that). The only message
I projected was – I am here, I came all this way, I am willing to back myself. And
so, I discovered, they were willing to back me too. It was a gutsy move. But I'm
here for a big game!

There are other famous examples of entrepreneurs who've worked backwards,
so to speak, selling a promise at huge risk, but with huge rewards too. I give
instant kudos to anyone who is prepared to put their arse on the line in this way.
If you can't back yourself, who else will? When I was carrying out interviews for
an advertising executive to join our team, I met a girl who was very nice and very
experienced, but she was asking for AU$130,000 a year, which at the time was way
out of our budget. So I told her – I can't make that your set wage, however, I can
put you on a high commission structure so that if you bring in enough deals that
would easily be within your bracket and then some. If she had faith in her ability
she would have jumped at the opportunity. But she didn't. So why should I take
the risk of employing her?

When I'm looking for people to join me on my entrepreneurial journey –
whether it's staff members, distributors, producers, retailers or sponsors – I want
someone who will share my vision and it is up to us, as the idea-makers, to not
build a prototype but a portal, so they can cast their mind forwards and see its
future potential.

HOW TO SET UP A START-UP ON A SHOESTRING

KEEP YOUR OVERHEADS LOW

For me this means relying on an army of freelancers to use when and, most importantly, if we need them rather than having a large in-house team whose skills might not always be required day after day, but whom you're always paying (more on this in chapter eight on risk and resilience). A freelancer might take two weeks or two hours to do a task, but it's not on your head (or your overheads) because you're paying them by project no matter how long that takes.

HIT THE GROUND RUNNING

As a small business you DO NOT have time to shuffle paper around. You need to start selling from day one. No exceptions. If you doubt your idea perhaps its better to put a pin in it and pursue another idea that you can believe in. As I wrote in *Daring & Disruptive* and elaborated on in this chapter, I see many start-ups make the mistake of pumping money into prototypes, testing and elaborate business plans before they even know if an idea has legs. Test early, seek out brutal feedback and be prepared to move on if you need to.

PAY IN PERKS

We ran an article early on around the topic of "start-up slumber parties" about companies, such as World Lister in the US, that instead of paying staff a wage, rented a huge house for staff to live in rent-free and supplied food for their team. According to the founder, this was far cheaper than paying multiple salaries, and all of his team utterly loved living together (hmmm, not sure this would be for everyone). It might have helped that the shared house was on the edge of the beach with its own jetty.

LEVERAGE – ANYTHING!

In all my books I talk about the importance of value exchange because it is so important. What do you have to offer that's non-monetary? In this day and age it's all about attention. How can you boost someone else's profile using your product or service, and how can this be leveraged to convince them to build a partnership? 'Value exchange' are the two most important words we have lived by in growing our brand.

OVERESTIMATE EXPENSES, UNDERESTIMATE REVENUE

It might seem like a contradiction, but to have a long-running business you need to be an eternal optimist who plans for the worst-case scenario. When I launched my book *Daring & Disruptive*, I was prepared to make a loss and budgeted accordingly. What a surprise when it started to bring in AU$7000 a week of unexpected revenue (just from our web sales alone).

PIGGYBACK ON POWER

If you're selling a product, don't wait until you have the funds to build a website, instead leverage the ready-made community of sites like Amazon, Ebay and Etsy. They're the perfect place to road test a product with minimal risk and also offer data on your demographic, such as the countries where most of the people viewing your items live, which means you can tailor your marketing accordingly.

Dreams
for sale.
only serious offers accepted.

Chapter 6
Good Fortune

I once asked a prominent businessman, maybe the most prominent businessman in Australia, why he does what he does. Why do you get up every day to lead a cast of thousands? Why do you run a business that trades, sells, barters and bargains? Why do you get out of bed with the sole purpose of turning your existing money into more money? I looked him straight in the eye – and he couldn't answer me.

After a kind of awkward silence, where I didn't let him off the hook, this man, a multimillionaire who runs business seminars and appears on television shows, finally answered. "I don't know," he shrugged his shoulders, "I just do" and in that moment I instantly lost respect for him. It might sound harsh, but he was the perfect example of the type of character that unfortunately you do come across quite a lot in the business world – ego-driven business people who haven't really looked into themselves and examined their reason for being on this planet, or been brave enough to ask themselves why they're making money. They just know they want to make a lot of it. As quickly as possible.

You'll have figured out by now that I have absolutely nothing against the idea of making money. I am pro-profit. I love money if – and this is a big if – you know what your purpose and your 'why' is. In an ideal world, that purpose should be a feeling rather than an object, or at least a feeling caused by an object. If you say to me, "I want to make $2.5 million by my 31st birthday" then I'll doubt that you'll do it. I'll believe you a little more if you say, "I want to make $2.5 million by my 31st birthday so I can buy a super yacht." However, if you turn around and say, "I want to make $2.5 million by my 31st birthday so I can buy a super yacht because I love the feeling of freedom and adventure that you get on the ocean" then I'm sure I'll see your name on the BRW Rich List by your third decade.

As I often say, my 'why' when it comes to *The Collective* is to create a community of like-minded game-changers who can lift, motivate, inspire and celebrate each other, to live out loud, as the biggest, boldest version of themselves. Well, as the founder of that movement I have to lead by example, and it would be at odds with my message if I financially shrank and never allowed myself to celebrate, to invest, to sow the seeds and reap the rewards spent!

Just for now, I don't want to talk about charitable giving and paying it forward because it's such an important component that I'm going to dedicate an entire chapter to it. Instead, here, I want to focus on personal spending and how we can trade money for happiness. Yes, I've said it, because I do believe it. While saving money is of course important, I also truly believe there is a time and a place for conscious, constructive, considered spending that enables you to live your life fully, to thrive, strive, expand, enjoy and generally be happy.

"How sad to see a father with money and no joy," said the American entrepreneur Jim Rohn. "The man studied economics, but never studied happiness." To be a successful entrepreneur I believe you need a grasp of both – financial literacy and a sense of fun, fascination and clear understanding of what makes you and your loved ones shine. Why do you want to make money and how do you want your life to change for the better once you have it? When you type "can money buy happiness?" into Google there are over 56,600,000 results for the question. Clearly, a lot of people want to know the answer to it, with countless surveys, studies and snippets of anecdotal evidence that often seem to contradict each other. On the pro-money side, a 2013 study from the University of Michigan found that happiness does seem to increase with salary (only 43 per cent of people earning between US$20,000 and US$30,000 describe themselves as "very happy" but in the US$250,000–US$500,000 bracket 83 per cent of people do).

But it's not a clear case, as there is conflicting evidence and studies measure different indicators of happiness. A well-known study from 2010 found day-to-day contentment and daily mood increases only up until a salary of US$75,000 while happiness with one's overall place in the world keeps increasing with income. A 2011 study from Boston College's Center on Wealth and Philanthropy surveyed 165 households with assets of US$25 million or more and found they were "generally dissatisfied" and said their money contributed to deep anxieties around love, work and family. What were their biggest worries? They felt they had "lost the right to complain about anything for fear of sounding – or being – ungrateful" and also worried their children would become "trust-fund brats" because of their inheritances.

I know, I know, it can be hard to be sympathetic when there are people in the world who can't afford to feed their children and yet, I'm sure that to the entrepreneur who complains that he'll "only" make $2.3 million this year his concerns are very real. Just as the millionaire who has to postpone his private jet flight due to an inconvenient ash cloud really does feel hard done by!

"There's nothing worse than a rich person who's chronically angry or unhappy," says motivational speaker Tony Robbins, "There's really no excuse for it, yet I see this phenomenon so often. It's the result of an extremely unbalanced life, one with too much expectation and not enough appreciation for what's already there." There's even a diagnosis to describe it – Sudden Wealth Syndrome – coined by psychologist Stephen Goldbart and Joan DiFuria to depict the stress, guilt, sleep disorders and identity confusion that can accompany a big windfall.

I recently witnessed this happen to someone close to me and the fallout was so sad. To see someone so kind, so generous, with a beautiful, big, authentic 'why' and a vision to change the world turn into an ego-maniac who wanted to cast aside the person who loved him the most was heartbreaking. How many people with money never think they have enough of it and are constantly moving their goalposts, never satisfied and forever hungry for more? Why do so many wealthy people appear to be unhappy and, most importantly, how will you ensure that you're not one of them? How will you ensure that money motivates and drives you, without making you mean and ungrateful? How can money be your 'why' without it being your whine? Because at the end of the workday, what is the point of working, pushing, striving, thriving and sacrificing, if the pot of gold at the end of your rainbow doesn't light up your sky?

OOPS, DID I BUY THAT?

A few months after launching *The Collective*, when we moved back into our new, shiny headquarters after renovation, I decided to buy a treadmill to keep in the office. I'm an exercise fiend and I thought being able to do a workout while holding meetings sounded like a great idea. I also thought it was a great idea to spend AU$1600 on a super-duper, high-tech, bells-and-whistles model, even though at that point I was using a laptop nicknamed "the tank" because I insisted I couldn't afford an upgrade.

But, the treadmill was an investment, right? I kept repeating this as the delivery man put it together on the office balcony, right in front of the floor-to-ceiling glass window of the marketing department. Who doesn't want their boss running on a treadmill right in front of them as they're trying to work? Yet, they needn't have worried because as I type this two years later, the treadmill has never been turned on. Not once. Not ever. However, it has been rained on incessantly, so is now ruined to the point that we can't even sell it. And it's so heavy that none of my team would be capable of lifting it, which means that I'll have to pay someone to dismantle and remove it (unless any of you would like to volunteer?).

Why am I telling you this? Because it's an example of the trap many of us fall into if we don't constantly check in with our 'why' when it comes to earning, spending, splurging, saving and scrimping. I'm glad in a sense that the treadmill is almost impossible to move because it serves as a personal reminder of how not to throw away money. I'm not saying a treadmill is a bad purchase, in fact, it would be a perfect personal investment for some people. But for me it was totally irrelevant to my 'why'. I bought it in a moment of excitement because I was determined to jump-start a revamped fitness regime, even though it was totally at odds with my true self (for a nature lover like me running on a treadmill is not all that enjoyable, as I'd far rather be outside feeling the grass under my feet).

I love the quote from American author James W Frick who says, "Don't tell me where your priorities are. Show me where you spend your money and I'll tell you what they are." I truly believe that money can make people happy if people learn to both earn it and spend it in line with their true purpose, values and ethos. On the flip side, money can trigger huge unhappiness if the income and outgoings of their revenue streams are out of alignment with who they really are.

There are multiple studies that show spending money on experiences brings more immediate and enduring happiness than purchasing an inanimate object. I'm not going to tell you what your 'why' should be – you know it deep down, when you peel away the layers of peer pressure, social expectation and the buzz of television adverts, and hook into the things that really make your heart sing.

It's important to me that all my purchases align with my passions. Perfectly. Otherwise I get into a buy-fast, regret-later treadmill situation, when I could have used that AU$1600 to take my team on a creative excursion that would have been far more beneficial.

This wasn't always the case – I used to spend money to fill a void in my life because I felt a little empty and directionless. I was an advertiser's dream. I'm sure a lot of people can identify! But now I really do despise 'stuff'. This is why when making purchases, I constantly check, analyse and deconstruct my thought process. Why do I want to spend this? Is it because it will bring me genuine emotional, psychological, physical or educational benefits or are social expectations, peer pressure or a childhood imprint driving this desire? This also applies to not spending money. We all have different blockages (for me, I cringe

MONEY & MINDFULNESS

at the idea of spending money on furniture although I can't explain why). If you have the internal monologue "I can't afford that..." it's important to check yourself and ask: is this true? Do you actually have the money? In which case, what is stopping you wanting to spend it on a certain item or experience?

I shudder at the thought of spending $2 on a bottle of water, partly as an imprint from my childhood and partly because I think it's unnecessary when we're so lucky to have clean drinking water on tap in free supply (although I make an exception for those who use it for good, like our dear friends from Thankyou). My friends know that if we go out to dinner with a group I'm happy to split the bill any which way but I won't pay for alcohol. After over 10 years of not drinking it doesn't sit well with me to pay for a substance that was once my demon. Yet, I recently hired a private seaplane to take a friend and I on a day trip to one of my favourite restaurants on Sydney's northern beaches, flying in over the Opera House. Was it worth it? Yes, especially to see their amazement as we flew in over the glittering water of the harbour. Do you have to agree with my purchase? No, because at the end of the day it's my money, my emotional investment and my everlasting memories.

There have been times in my life when I've been in the fortunate situation of having money, but also times in my life where I've had absolutely nothing, and I now realise the difference in my happiness levels doesn't really correlate to the number that flashes up on an ATM screen but rather, how I chose to spend that money. A banknote has no worth until you use it for a purpose and then, from the paper, create a beautiful origami sculpture.

The goal isn't money.
The goal is living life
on your terms.

— Chris Brogan

SMILES FOR SALE.
BUY ONE GET ONE FREE!

If you had all the money you ever needed, what would you be doing with your life right now? Someone posted this question on the anonymous message sharing website Whisper and, at the time of my writing this, it had more than 5600 responses – some funny, some shocking, some heartbreaking. Here are just a few examples:

- Creating a 'tinier house movement' village that'll [have] extremely affordable housing and [be] self-sufficient. (even been working on plans so I'm prepared)
- Protecting my son from his insane father
- Exactly what I'm already doing! I feel very fortunate
- Start believing in myself and become somebody
- Create our own private Eden just outside the city: an antique farmhouse [and] vineyard with moonflowers and clematis, with gardens, orchards and a barn modified into an aviary and hand-feeding nursery
- I'd go, me and two beloved friends, study classical singing in Italy, and I'd never more teach so many classes
- Why should I fantasise about something that isn't going to happen?
- Sitting on some beach with a tiny umbrella in my drink and a hot chick next to me
- Sitting in a loft writing and planning my three-month long vacation across Europe
- I would do nothing, and it would be everything I could hope it would be
- I'd buy all the McDonalds and then SHUT THEM DOWN!
- Pay off my debt and start fresh. I wouldn't let anyone know I had money and

live a normal life without worry and help my family and friends when needed
- Purchase 51 per cent of every major corporation in the US, develop a more efficient US healthcare system and invest the rest in BitCoin virtual currency
- I will build a place where I can attend to all the people in need and meet their needs so that my name will not be forgotten
- Living with my toes in the sand
- I'd be doing my dream job because I would have been able to pay for uni (sad face), [I] so want to be an air-traffic controller
- Travel the world on my own terms. And probably buy a new truck
- I would teach technology to kids…
- Let my mum retire, learn to fly, go on mission trips with my family
- I would buy more pets, the latest iPhone and a personal assistant for my mum
- Ceramics
- I would get nose surgery
- Buy an island then let my friends and family live there too
- Trying to have a baby with IVF or adopting. Both are expensive…
- Become a nomad, learn everything I possibly could
- I would be Batman

Even though some of the above are tongue in cheek (I think), it's still an interesting snapshot into human psychology, different dreams, ideals, desires and the value that different people of different backgrounds place on priceless opportunities. Has this long list inspired you? Then take a moment to consider this question – if I handed you a big wad of $100 notes right now, what purchase, place or person flashes into your mind?

I'm not going to tell you exactly how much money I'm giving you because wealth is so subjective and means different values to different people. But, let's just say there is a lot of cash there. An awful lot. What do you imagine when I hand you the windfall? A shiny new car, a plane ticket to see your long-distance parent, a house deposit that offers security or a new diamond collar for your puppy? There is no right or wrong answer. But it's an interesting experiment, as I believe that how you spend money is just as much a mark of your passion, your ethos and your purpose, as how you earned it in the first place. Don't overthink it, just the first light-bulb thought…

In *Daring & Disruptive* I devote an entire chapter to the importance of investing in yourself, whether it's paying $9.95 for a magazine that will inspire you, $1200 for a conference or eye-watering rent for an inspiring office space because you know in the long-term it will make you more productive. I recently met a tech entrepreneur who told me he puts aside six per cent of his salary every year for self-development, whether that means doing a course, booking a yoga retreat, learning a language or even – as was the case last year – using the money to pay for a meal-delivery service for four weeks. How is this self-development? It was the month leading up to the launch of new software and he knew that he was so busy, if he didn't pay for healthy meals to be delivered then he wouldn't eat properly and would therefore feel more stressed and less capable. It shows that an investment in self-development doesn't have to mean buying a book; it can mean anything to anyone.

This is why I never try to judge anyone at the upper end of the wealth spectrum for purchases that might seem indulgent to some. As I mentioned in chapter two, all too often, especially in the start-up sector, we can be in danger of glorifying poverty (the start-up founder who sleeps on his friend's couch) but why shouldn't those who've 'made it' reap the rewards?

Take the example of Mark Zuckerberg, who was once described as the "poorest rich person I've ever seen in my life" by his university alumnus Tyler Winklevoss, for living in a beaten-up rental apartment even when Facebook was worth millions. Is the Facebook founder any less dedicated to his business, now that he owns a house in Palo Alto, California, reported to be worth US$10 million (not to mention its four neighbouring properties, for which he collectively paid over US$30 million)? Likewise, is Sheryl Sandberg extravagant for building a six-bedroom, six-bathroom property in Menlo Park? It has a gym, wine room, movie theatre and 'living roof' covered in plants and flowers, which can't have come cheap. Let's look at the message these extras send out. I think the owner of this house wants a place she can wind down, relax and enjoy herself. A place she can spend time with her family, in nature and ensure her life has balance. This is perfectly aligned with Sheryl Sandberg, who famously told an interviewer she always leaves the office at 5.30pm on the dot to be at home with her children for dinner, even if she admits to opening up her laptop once they're asleep.

To me, this is how to spend money the right way, with purchases or experiences that support, remind and enable your life purpose, ethos and ethics. It's the same reason I have a personal trainer, even though I once saw it as indulgent, because when I do speaking gigs I tell people that I prioritise health above all else and I know that without a trainer I'd be prone to skip a workout when times are busy (which is always). It's why I spend a lot of money on travel, because I believe it boosts creativity, widens your eyes and makes you dream bigger. It's why I pay for office space with a balcony and huge windows, because I need lightness and brightness to feel inspired, even though my rent is kind of extortionate.

Can money buy happiness? If we spend within our means and always, always check our intention before making a purchase, it can help. Look at the last five purchases you put on your credit card. Were they made to truly enhance your life, to boost your happiness, health, enjoyment or productiveness, or that of people you care about? Or did another factor come into play – was the purchase made to impress, to prove a point, to belittle or out of pressure to conform or pass expectations?

What were the last three purchases on my credit card? They were AU$1200 for two flights to Hayman Island as a birthday treat, AU$70 on a physiotherapy appointment because I've been having issues with my ankle and payment to a team of house removalists who recently helped me pack up and move my worldly possessions to my new house. I managed to perfectly time moving day with *The Collective*'s monthly print deadline (oops!) and so made the choice to outsource so I didn't have to abandon my team to pack and then unpack boxes. Incidentally, it was one of the best AU$59 I have ever spent. As a rule of thumb, all of my purchases support my purpose, although I still make the odd 'treadmill buy' sometimes when I forget to check in with my 'why' and buy from a place of ego, stress or peer pressure.

Money can support, amplify and scale other factors in life that genuinely do make you happy. It can enable you to fly your family across the country to attend your birthday party, to pay for a friend to have weekly reiki when they're in chemotherapy, it can allow you to afford a house with enough space for a pet puppy, which brings joy and comfort to you and your family. Some might argue these purchases – any purchases – are feeding the 'corporate machine', but this money is spent with the best intention and a true, heartfelt purpose. To me this is what living in a place of abundance is all about – adding a sparkly, gold sheen to your everyday life.

DOES STUFF SATISFY YOU?

This is a column I wrote in an early issue of *The Collective*. As the brand has grown, my profile has increased and I'm lucky to have more disposable income than ever, I can hand-on-heart say I only believe in this sentiment more. I wrote this column in Issue 13 and now, with more than twice that number of issues, it could not be more true…

"For the past six weeks I have pretty much worn the same outfit. I don't mean in an unwashed, skanky kind of way. But a variance of black pants or leggings, black tee, black knee-high boots and black leather jacket. Every single day and night, amping it up for more formal occasions and chilling it right down for my beloved training sessions.

That's my first observation for the month. The second is about the stuff in my life. I used to buy heaps and heaps of stuff for the house and office but for some reason, I've stopped. Wracking my brain, I think it would be six months since I purchased something just to decorate a part of my life. And in my job, I do get given loads of stuff (which I love and am truly grateful for) but unless it has an immediate practical use, I try and give it all away.

There's also a third. I decided to move house recently and as the moving date drew close, I suggested to my partner that part of me wanted to be homeless. He looked puzzled. What I meant was that I wanted to be free, unencumbered and liberated with two suitcases to my name. I loved the notion of putting everything into storage and bunking down in someone's spare room for a while.

I hadn't joined the dots until that point. I'm wearing the same clothes on rotation, I'm not buying anything new and I have a hankering to have no fixed address. No, I'm not sick or depressed! I'm focused. And my partner was the one who pointed it out, suggesting I was channelling the late Steve Jobs or Mark Zuckerberg, who have been known for their minimalist attire especially in high-growth phases. Steve was famous for his black turtlenecks and according to his biographer, Walter Isaacson, he owned 100 of the same Issey Miyake sweater.

When you're running a multibillion-dollar company across 38 countries, who has time for extra decision-making? As for the Facebook founder, Mark is known for having 20 identical grey T-shirts that are worn on rotation with blue jeans and trainers. Whether it was said in jest or complete seriousness, it was music to my ears. Who doesn't want to be likened to some of the greats on the entrepreneurial journey?"

To win without risk is

to triumph without glory.

—Pierre Corneille

Chapter 7

Perception versus Reality

I n Issue 17 of *The Collective*, we interviewed Nikki Durkin, the founder of the clothes-swapping service 99dresses, shortly after she was forced to close her start-up. With amazing courage, she announced the closure in a heartbreaking blog post titled 'My start-up failed and this is what it feels like...', which was read by over 200,000 people in three days as readers reached out with sympathy and to say they could relate to her problems.

"Over 90 per cent of tech start-ups fail, but I never thought my baby, 99dresses, would be one of them," wrote Nikki, "We had users and traction, then we fell off a cliff. My four-year emotional rollercoaster just came to an end." In a subsequent post she reflects, "99dresses was the love I'd married as a teenage bride with all the naivety and optimism of youth. We'd grown together, evolved. She was part of me and this was her eulogy."

I remember reading that blog and being just as shocked as the people who left comments, because like many of them I was under the impression 99dresses was doing brilliantly, rising, thriving and prospering. I knew the company had raised over AU$635,000 in funding since its launch, I'd watched its social media community grow and heard about so many clothes swapping events.

Just a month or two before its closure was announced, I'd seen Nikki tweeting about her perfect week, where she'd spoken at a tech conference, gone to a 7.30am pre-work dance party (they do that in New York City) and had a brainstorming brunch in an amazing rooftop restaurant. Her twit-pics looked amazing, not at all indicative of an entrepreneur on the brink of bankruptcy. But this is where the 'perception versus reality' of money, especially in the start-up sphere, comes into play. To a degree, in her own words, she was faking it.

"Whenever I'd log onto Facebook, I see posts from friends who run start-ups launching new products on TechCrunch, announcing their new fundraising rounds or acquisition, and posting photos of their happy teams," explained Nikki when we interviewed her.

"I'm only realising now that some of this is an illusion. If you'd looked at my Twitter feed, even the week before we announced we were shutting, you'd have thought we were winning. I wasn't lying – I was just putting a spin on things.

"If you are running a business you have to fake it until you make it. It's a self-fulfilling prophecy – if you act like you are successful you are more likely to be. If you admit you're not doing well, you won't do well. It's a game you have to play."

Is this true? Well, let's look at my own situation. Every week I get emails from people asking me to invest in their companies and I fall on the floor laughing, not because their business ideas are bad (some are genius!) but because they actually believe that I have a spare few million dollars. "We just need AU$750,000 to fund our prototype/conference/global press tour and would love *The Collective* to be the primary sponsor." I've been known to snort into my green smoothie. It's hilarious to me, but in a way it's also a sign that I'm doing my job well.

Because here is the slightly inconvenient truth – *The Collective* magazine itself, at this point, just over three years into its infancy, is not making a profit. Oh, we're selling like hotcakes but as I previously mentioned, I wanted to offer it at a reasonable price tag and so, once you subtract an average of AU$350,000 in production costs we're pretty much breaking even. I can understand if you're surprised by the statement because from the outside the magazine is a glossy, glamorous symbol of substance, with the nod of approval from cover stars like George Clooney, Ryan Gosling, Amy Poehler and Anna Kendrick, and members of my team reporting from all manner of ritzy events like the Oscars and Paris Fashion Week. As my social media feed shows, I spend my life jetting to exotic locations for speaking gigs or simply for pleasure because I believe that travel triggers the imagination. But, no, the print magazine does not make a profit. So how do I continue to live a high life? Two reasons. 1) *The Collective* brand does make a profit as a business overall thanks to the multiple web of systems, processes, strategies and side projects, the books, events, consultations, sponsorships and collaborations that I cushion our income with. 2) The surplus money I do have I spend on the magazine, to ensure it's the optimal quality for readers, advertisers and everyone who contributes to it. And it's a hairy high risk I still juggle every single day.

I've known of many magazines where, to cut costs and encourage profit, they swap to a cheaper paper quality, even if the writing blurs or the pictures smudge. I've heard of global corporations where they no longer buy birthday cakes for staff or supply milk and tea bags because they think it's a waste of money. Should I take these measures to increase our chances of profit? I choose not to, because it's totally at odds with my brand's message. As I've said consistently, I'm all about living the fullest, most vibrant version of your life, and so I live just slightly above my means. Always. Unapologetically. And I'm not the only one. Kelly Lovell's Huffington Post article, 'I'm not cheap, I'm an entrepreneur', sums up the financial illusion of many start-ups brilliantly. Kelly writes about the different demographics that typically have debt – the struggling artist and the student – but suggests we need to add a third – the hard-working entrepreneur. "Yet unlike a student in debt, an entrepreneur's lifestyle isn't as transparent. Depending on the line of work, entrepreneurs can be found to travel, attend special events, have influential colleagues and so on. They can hold fancy titles like 'CEO' and 'President', and have responsibilities of running companies. On the outside their lives can seem a lot more glamorous or successful than they are. The hard reality is most entrepreneurs are struggling and can be just as poor as a student."

Let me add a disclaimer. I am definitely NOT (sorry to shout but this is important) saying that you should rack up hundreds of thousands worth of debt and dig yourself into a hole you may never get out of. But it comes back to the conscious, calculated spending choices that we discussed in Chapter Six, which covered money and happiness. I do not spend with reckless abandon but I always

Before you speak, listen.

    Before you write, think.

Before you spend, earn.

Before you invest, investigate

Before you criticise, wait.

Before you pray, forgive.

Before you quit, try.

    Before you retire, save.

      Before you die, give.

— William A Ward

want my brand to appear bigger than our means – and one day hopefully our bottom line will catch up with it.

This might seem like a slightly irresponsible attitude but I don't spend money recklessly. However, I also refuse to be trapped in a mindset of scarcity. I've heard Steve Jobs described as a "multiplier" – someone who can unlock the intelligence and latent potential in the people around him, as opposed to a "diminisher", who is someone who reduces other people's power. Well, I aim to be a multiplier in all aspects of my business, operating like a billionaire on a start-up budget, taking a tiny spark and turning it into a field of flashing fireworks.

Years ago, when I was reading the self-help book *The Secret* by Rhonda Byrne, one paragraph really stuck with me in which she wrote, "You are a magnet. When you become a magnet of wealth, you attract wealth. When you become a magnet of health, you attract health. When you become magnet of love, you attract love. When you become a magnet of joy, you attract joy. You must become the magnet of whatever it is you want, to bring it to you."

Was Nikki of 99dresses wrong for projecting a profitable facade even though her company was about to collapse? I don't think so. I have to make choices every single day about what to spend money on – AU$9500 for one photo for the magazine, AU$14,000 to shoot an in-demand A-lister, AU$21,000 to do an embellishment on the front cover. I don't always say yes, but I don't always say no either because some are an investment in my brand's future. I believe Nikki is right, sometimes you have to fake it until you make it. That's why this book is more about mindset than spreadsheets. I believe that like attracts like and if you project success, wealth and happiness you are far more likely to attract it. Okay, at the moment the magazine itself, my 'hero product', is not so much a cash cow as a little lamb that needs constant nursing and coaxing to keep growing. But one day, I have utter faith that it will be big and strong enough to provide milk to feed us all or at the very least it will be the cornerstone from which other products and services can hold their own and will flow.

HOW TO FAKE PROFIT UNTIL YOU MAKE PROFIT

USE ALTERNATIVE CURRENCY:

Don't have cash in the bank? What do you have to barter with? I know a tech entrepreneur who was also a keen hiker with expert knowledge of the Australian bush. He needed a lawyer to help him write a patent. He couldn't afford the fee, so offered to take a group from the firm on a team-bonding day in a national park, teaching them survival skills and food forage. Your personal currency might not be related to your business, so think outside the box – or outside the city.

DO A SOFT LAUNCH FIRST:

When we produced the *Daring & Disruptive Playbook* I did a soft launch first – meaning I printed 500 copies of it as a test run in Australia and offered these on pre-sale to readers, promoting it through social media. If it didn't attract any interest I'd make the call not to do a further print run. Luckily, it sold its little socks off and we quickly went for a much larger offshore run. Another good strategy is to use the money from the sale of the soft launch to pay for a bells-and-whistles launch party when the product actually hits stores.

BUY NOW, PAY LATER:

I've already included a few examples of this strategy because it's one I come back to often, especially when I'm looking for distributors. Most companies do expect money up-front for services these days, but the secret to pulling this off is relentless enthusiasm and abounding self-belief (a proven track record is also helpful, but not essential). If you stock my product, I can't pay for placement, but I guarantee they will sell and you'll make X amount from the profit.

TRUTH AND TRANSPARENCY

Have you heard of the Internet craze 'Rich Kids of Instagram'? (Bear with me because this is relevant, I promise). It's a montage of photos that offspring of the top-tier percentile post on social media showcasing their excessive, everyday activities – lying in a solid gold bathtub, jumping out of a private helicopter into the ocean, showing off a US$21,050 bar bill spent on Grey Goose vodka in one evening.

But what I find even funnier – and far more relatable – are the parodies that people now post showing images from Rich Kids of Instagram versus what life really looks like for the rest of us. On one side a rich kid takes a photo standing on the bonnet of his Porsche... a normal guy takes a photo standing on the saddle of his bicycle. A rich kid takes a photo of himself lying in US$100 bills... a normal girl takes of photo of herself covered in fivers. A rich kid takes a photo holding a giant bottle of champagne... a normal girl takes a photo with one of those huge, plastic water bottles you find in water coolers.

There's a perception-versus-reality disparity around the concept of launching a start-up and the effort, investment and struggle it really takes to do it. You might love to believe that one day you'll bump into an investor in a café who will notice you typing out a business plan and BOOM, you're financial. Likewise, in an ideal world, every crowdfunding campaign will make a fortune, every product will be noticed by Oprah and every income will be passive so that we can retire to Saint-Tropez. But the reality is this happens to the minority, and setting up a start-up is usually far less glamorous than the urban myths. You're far more likely to be living on cornflakes than caviar.

As I write this, a prominent businessman who I also count as a friend owes me AU$19,000. It's a long story, and I hope you don't mind that I won't share it, because it's not really relevant to the point I'm going to make anyway. Needless to say, he owes me AU$19,000 and has admitted he won't be at liberty to pay me back anytime soon. But the really interesting fact, which may surprise you, is this is a guy with a company valued at US$31 million. Over the years, you won't imagine how many clients I've worked with whose net worth is estimated at millions – by the media and by themselves – and yet behind the scenes they have very private conversations with me saying they are very sorry, but they can't pay their bills this month. It's tricky because although I'm the first to say our brand is bigger than our bottom line, I am also careful to respect my responsibilities to my staff, freelancers and anyone who works with me. I'm not a fan of 'boogey' money.

I will also strive to tell the truth if another entrepreneur asks me directly about how prosperous my business is. While I get the fake-it-till-you-make-it thing, I also think it's vital that we, within the start-up scene, have fair comparisons and don't have false expectations about how much we should be making, spending, losing and saving to reach our end goal. This is also the reason that I am extremely open with my own team about the finances of the company. Some might say too open, but I think it's imperative that leaders educate their teams on the ins and outs of business and what it costs to keep the door open. This goes for the senior advertising staff all the way through to our editorial assistant – everyone. I have a big white board in the kitchen where anyone can read about the revenue we bring in for each issue, from advertising, marketing and sponsorship deals. I am also very open about our outgoings, and will talk numbers, stats and figures without censorship in our open plan office.

This is because I want the team to understand my decisions, and those of the executive team, if we say a particular photograph is too expensive to buy right now, or it's not the right time to employ another staff member or why I think an idea for a book series is a great one, but not financially viable at the moment. I am all too aware that just as the outside world sees my Instagram photos of me holidaying on Necker Island and chairing a conference at a luxury health retreat, my team also sees these snapshots. I never want them to think that I'm just off on a junket spending the company's money (this perception-versus-reality strategy can backfire sometimes). And so I educate them – that trip to Necker was a long-term networking strategy, that health retreat paid me AU$12,000 to speak to attendees and bought 100 copies of my book at the same time. I have a policy of transparency with my team who I trust implicitly (and who also sign confidentially agreements because you still can't be too careful, no matter how much you love people).

Here's an example of why transparency is so important within a company. Years ago, well before *The Collective*, in my book publishing business one of my team members, who was on a AU$35,000-a-year salary, questioned how we were being paid AU$25,000 to develop some sales material for a client. How could her entire salary be close to one single job we were doing for someone else? She just didn't get it... I could understand her confusion, and so I decided to take her through an exercise. We would work on this project together, so she could see every stage of the process, from brainstorming to design to creation to distribution and every teeny, tiny tweak in between. Well, fast-forward three months and endless changes (this client was a particularly tricky one who kept changing their mind) later, she got it... What may appear like a simple task from the outside was WAY more complex, time-consuming and all-encompassing than she'd realised. Her attitude completely changed and suddenly she was saying, "Oh my goodness, we should be charging them 10 times that much!" Coincidentally, she was right – and as I've said in earlier chapters, we eventually did.

There is a lot of smoke and mirrors when it comes to building a brand and finding the resources to balance the books of a business. Just remember that not everything you see on social media, for example, is necessarily accurate – and be sure to talk the truth about money with the people who matter.

Keep your face always
toward the sunshine
and the shadows will
fall behind you.

— Walt Whitman

The happiest people don't
have the best of everything,
they just make the best of
everything, they have.

—Unknown

THE SALARY CEILING

As your brand grows, scales and (hopefully) gets on the global radar, you can find yourself in a tricky situation if your bottom line hasn't caught up – your staff may (will!) be poached by companies with more money than you have to offer. It's a compliment to your success, really.

When I began *The Collective* nearly all of my team came to me with little or no magazine experience, but I took a punt on them, recognising their natural talent and skills in other fields. By working at the magazine, most learned, grew and thrived. Cue our competitors, who look at our brand, read our masthead and reach out to my team. We can offer you this much to jump ship…

I would love to say that none are tempted because we're just so lovable, but the reality is that no matter how amazing you make your work culture, even when you create a Zen-ful office and the team sees each other as family, money still talks and in some seasons of life is a key deciding factor. I understand that even the most loyal staff can be lured by a substantial salary (among other things).

We've had it recently where staff who were on about AU$50,000 were approached by other companies who were unashamedly in love with our brand and swooped in to offer them a salary of AU$70,000 and beyond for a more junior position. What can you do?

NUMBER 1: Do not take it personally (and this is a tricky one). You have two choices really – match the wage or admit you just can't do it, bid them farewell and look for an equally talented replacement.

NUMBER 2: Get even. I have on a rare occasion agreed to match a salary even though it's way above my budget. Sometimes you just have to bite your lip if an employee is worth it. Do I want the headache of having to find someone equally competent and also watch all that knowledge and internal experience walk out the door? Or would our energy be better spent doing what we do best?

NUMBER 3: Create an entrepreneurial spirit within your employees so they become intrapreneurs and have the opportunity to run 'mini companies' within your company. Encourage them to think of new revenue streams or product ideas and offer them commission or alternative revenue if they sell over a certain amount.

NUMBER 4: Use it as motivation to become bigger and more profitable. It comes back to your 'why' – I need to make money so that I can keep the talent I adore. Every time another company tries to poach my team, it puts a fire in my belly and a bomb under me to make *The Collective* even more successful so I can reward my team members. If the only factor making staff leave is money, then we need to make more money, which comes back to what your motivation is. We need to make money as a company so I can hold onto my top talent, who – as much as they love the brand – also have bills to pay.

Chapter 8

Risk + Resilience

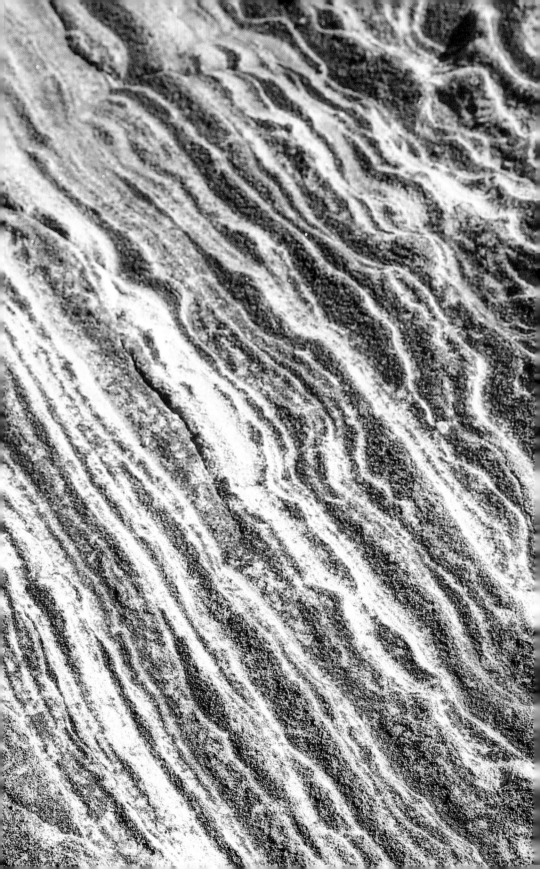

Remember earlier in this book when I confessed there have been times when my financial worries have reduced me to a sobbing, snot-strewn pity-party on the couch, because I was convinced we were going under? The last time that happened, which was thankfully back in the first year of *The Collective,* I woke up the next morning and made a decision – I'm going to hire six more staff members. Yes, I said hire rather than fire, which I think is the opposite reaction of most corporations with money worries. It might seem counterintuitive to you, when I was already sweating about how to afford my existing salaries, but this is how I run my businesses. A lot of people would have said I was crazy, but I sensed I was so close to success and just needed a bigger army. And so I added to my sales team, I took on board experienced and imaginative content creators who I knew could work fast, with flair, efficiency and innovation (this is the perfect blend I look for in team members). Their combined salaries added up to over AU$365,000 on my bottom line per year, which was no small subtraction for a start-up. But it paid off in every sense, as here we are, bigger, better, thriving, striving and winning. It was a risk, but as a very clever entrepreneur once told me, "It's a lack of risk-taking that leads to stagnation." The trick is learning the level of risk you're comfortable taking, and this cut-off point is personal – it depends on your resilience and experiences. It might sound odd but I know that to remain inspired, I need a certain amount of instability because it keeps me at the top of my game and drives me forwards.

Even publishing the first in this trilogy of books, *Daring & Disruptive,* was a massive risk for me financially. An initial run of 10,000 copies costs about AU$150,000 to produce, and then there's the time zap on my staff who have to jump in to edit my rambling, lay out the pages, arrange distribution and launch events across the country (I don't do things by halves). But, this risk was within my comfort zone because it was a project I was so excited about, a topic I was so passionate about, and something that I felt I owed to our readers, that if it hadn't sold then, hell, I would have given the whole crate away for free, just to share it with people. Of course, I was far more delighted when within the first month it made over AU$33,000 in sales, and we rapidly hit 'print' on another 10,000 copies. This doesn't mean I always get it right – some other books that I've published have sold only 500 copies. But, that doesn't stop me jumping back on the horse (or back on the bookshelf) and trying again...

When Mike Cannon-Brookes, the co-founder of successful software start-up Atlassian, was asked about his top advice for entrepreneurs he said, "If you can't smell burning, you're not sniffing hard enough," meaning that every groundbreaking start-up is going to come up against problems, riffs, tiffs and challenges on the path to greatness. Running your own business isn't for the faint-hearted and should come with a level of risk. In fact, I'd say risk is vital, but the good news is you can build up resilience like you never thought possible.

A study published in June 2014 by the Halle Institute for Economic Research found that people who choose to become self-employed are not necessarily more naturally tolerant of risk than others. However, the research found that entrepreneurs do become more comfortable with risk over time. And though I'd be lying if I said that every risk pays off, that every stab in the dark hits its mark and every adventurer finds treasure, it does certainly happen.

If four small shopkeepers from Texas hadn't dreamt well above their means when they decided the world needed a healthy supermarket, then the Whole Foods Market chain wouldn't exist (the brand reported sales of US$14.2 billion in fiscal year 2014). When Google bought YouTube in 2006 for US$1.65 billion it was seen as a huge amount of money for a relatively untested tech platform that was, at the time, bringing in no revenue. In 2014, it was reported that Google generated US$4 billion in revenue from YouTube.

Unfortunately, not many start-ups are an overnight success. Even Sara Blakely had to toil away for years to get Spanx noticed before she caught the attention of Oprah, and within that limbo are-we-going-to-sink-or-swim period there is nothing more nerve-racking than watching your receivables and payables. The radio-streaming company Pandora had such a shaky start, its early employees worked without pay for two and a half years, according to MarketWatch, and the company even considered gambling at a local casino to stay afloat because it struggled to find investment. Compare this to their 2013 calendar year results, when revenue jumped 56 per cent on the previous year to US$637.9 million.

Of course, these risky decisions are at the eye-watering end of the numbers scale, but no matter how large or small your business, you will still, on a weekly, daily, hourly basis, have to make decisions that contain a certain amount of risk and could potentially (sorry to be the bearer of bad news) make or break you. It's just important you identify the boundaries of your comfort zone – both emotionally and financially – so that if the worst does happen you know you can bounce back from it.

"Our business in life is not to get ahead of others but to get ahead of ourselves," says Stewart B Johnson, "to break our own records, to outstrip our yesterdays by our today, to do our work with more force than ever before." After nearly 14 years in business I know the depths of the holes that I can climb out of, how I can construct a ladder to help me up again, even in a barren landscape. I knew that, with my book, I could afford to take the hit if it bombed. And I knew when I hired those extra staff members that if the very, very worst happened, I could always finally take on an investor. Even though this wouldn't be an ideal solution for me, at least I knew in that scenario I would be able to honour and pay them. Of course, you also have to consider external factors. The week I started writing this book, I learned that I had to move house because the place I rented was being sold – immediately. I also got a car repair bill for AU$2500 and had to foot a AU$9500 bill for one photograph for the magazine, after a photo shoot fell through at the last minute because the star got food poisoning from an undercooked chicken skewer. These things happen. So, when calculating your level of risk, put financial buffers in place – and then buffer those buffers with more buffers (we'll talk about the best way to do this at the end of the chapter).

But first I want you to dig deep and ask yourself – how close to the edge of the cliff am I willing to tiptoe? There is no right or wrong answer, as everyone's comfort zone will be different, depending on many outside factors and lifestyle circumstances. I fully appreciate that right now in my life I am not a parent, I do not have dependents, although I do think of my staff like family and take my responsibilities to shield and care for them seriously. What level of risk are you prepared to take, how wide is your comfort zone, and how much can you afford to lose? Really.

When I was a little girl, I used to test how long I could hold my breath in our local swimming pool and was always amazed that it was far longer than I thought I could. This is how I've handled my business dealings as an adult, unafraid to delve deeper, to stay submerged for just one second longer than I thought I should. There is nothing more wonderful than when you pierce the top of the water, take that first breath of air and your whole self fills up with the fresh oxygen of survival.

Tell the negative committee
that meets inside your head
to sit down and shut up.

-Ann Bradford

IT'S NOT ALL PLAIN 'SALEING'

The truth is in business the smallest mistake can have a huge, sometimes catastrophic, impact. Years ago, we went to print on a book published in partnership with a massive bank who, at the very last minute – I'm talking about the day we were going to press – decided they wanted to add a phone number to the back page. This was at the earlier stage of my business, we were rushing, weren't fastidious about processes and procedures so nobody noticed that one digit on the phone number was missing… until almost 50,000 copies were sent out to hundreds of distributors across the country. It might seem like a minor error, but when it's a bank's contact details, it could be the difference between them getting customers and not.

   In this kind of situation a publisher has two choices – to call back and pulp the entire batch of books and then reprint them correctly OR, and this is the path we opted for in the end, get all the incorrect books couriered to your office, open every box, print off 50,000 stickers with the correct phone number and pay someone to individually stick them over the faulty phone numbers on 50,000 copies. It was a logistical nightmare, especially as the books had to be back with retailers for launch, which was two days away. It still makes my stomach flip to think about it, but this is just one of many, many, MANY examples of similar situations I've had over the years. Not because my team are sloppy (quite the opposite – I know my attention to detail can be lax, so I purposefully hire people who can find a needle in a haystack) but because they are human and sometimes for a multitude of reasons, mistakes just happen. Accept it. Deal with it. Learn from it. Protect yourself from it.

   What can you do to shelter yourself, your brand, your business and, in the case of this book, your bank balance? Just as I've learned my level of resilience over the years, I've also learned the systems, strategies, tools and safety nets that can cushion me if catastrophe strikes, protect me from the fall-out – and even leave me in a better position because of the pitfall. Yes, that is possible too.

I've talked in the past about how I rely on an army of freelancers – at this point over 70 individuals across multiple skill sets in multiple countries across the world – because this keeps my bottom line in check and allows me to only employ them when I really need them. But it's also for added protection, because of the all-important phrase, "sign-offs". After the phone number incident, we realised that everyone in the production chain needed to be accountable for every typo, picture and page number, so that if something went awry we'd know where the buck lies (and who was footing the bill – us or them). From that point on every page of every single book went through a sign-off process. The writer had to approve it, my editor had to approve it, and most importantly the client had to approve it. Their little signature on the corner of a proof was my insurance policy so that, if something was out of place and we found out far too late, they had a choice whether to let it slide or pay for changes. I'm happy to say that mistakes don't happen often, but boy it makes it easier for me to sleep at night knowing that I have a safety raft to float on.

Also bear in mind that what may appear like a risky decision to you, may not be a risky decision to me because I have knowledge of that specific market and have traversed that rocky path before. Jeff Bezos, the founder and CEO of Amazon says, "Ninety-plus per cent of the innovation at Amazon is incremental and critical and much less risky. We know how to open new product categories. We know how to open new geographies. That doesn't mean that these things are guaranteed to work, but we have a lot of expertise and a lot of knowledge… All of these things based on our operating history are things that we can analyse quantitatively rather than to have to make intuitive judgments."

Of course, even if you're financially sheltered, it's still horrible when mistakes are made, no matter how tiny. I am a people-pleasing perfectionist so I utterly hate it when mistakes are made, even if they are so tiny and insignificant that a reader would gloss over them and it doesn't at all impact their enjoyment. Did you read my previous book *Life & Love*? If you had one of the very first editions, did you notice a random paragraph in the middle of the book that was printed in red ink? Go, get your copy, check it (and feel free to have a giggle at my expense!). It's just a random error that I've had to learn to live with every time I flick past that page. It doesn't bother me now – *grinds teeth* – and do you know that no one, not a single person, pointed it out (incidentally no one pointed out that I had a fiancé as well and he went the same way as the red paragraph). If only you had seen our staff at the moment of discovery – it was horrendous. But mistakes happen, especially to entrepreneurial veterans, and it's all about making the best of it. I'm just grateful it happened to one of my books and not to a client's – now that would have been interesting (and by interesting, I mean hellish and costly).

If the error was due to a third party, say the person producing your product, if you're a clever, savvy business person and a good negotiator, you might even come out of it in a good position. I remember printing a book years ago where the background colour of the front cover was meant to be a warm orange. We signed it off. It looked really good. But when the books arrived it was a biscuit brown. The printer gave us a credit of AU$30,000 as an apology but we all decided to put the product into the marketplace. It was fine for sale, it just wasn't what we wanted. At the time, biscuit brown became my new best friend. Why didn't we think of it! And, needless to say, that hurt money from the printer was a massive financial help too. So, all was well that ended well, when you look at it from a glass-half-full attitude and aren't overly attached to a set outcome.

I can say for sure that if I hadn't taken certain calculated risks in my career, if I hadn't followed my gut instead of standard guidelines and put my business on the line, I certainly wouldn't be where I am today, and I very much doubt you'd be reading a book written by me. I had to accept the reality years ago that I had two choices – either admit that I couldn't handle risk, move to a lovely teepee in Byron Bay and live as a hippie (it was tempting and I did consider it, believe me) or accept that instability is inevitable and actually learn to enjoy it. As Richard Branson says, "Every risk is worth taking as long as it's for a good cause and contributes to a good life."

HOW TO AIR-BAG YOUR BUSINESS

RANK YOUR CUSTOMERS

This is a tip I heard from the owner of a car repair company, who ranked his returning customers as A, B or C depending on how quickly they paid him. In peak season when he was overworked, he prioritised his A customers and took care of them first, as he knew they paid within 30 days so he would have a faster, steadier capital flow. Unfortunately, right or wrongly, there are some clients who you just know will pay late, and you will have to chase them. As long as you know this, you can manage your expectations (and at busy periods choose whether to take a job or politely say you'll have to pass on this particular project).

TAKE OUT INSURANCE

There are many options for different levels of business insurance that, just like health insurance, vary depending on the age, size and complexity of your company. As entrepreneurs it's important to think of the worst-case scenario – what if I got sick and was unable to work, what if the bottom dropped out of the market and we weren't able to pay our bills? I launched my first business just weeks after 9/11, which had a huge knock-on effect for all trades and showed me sometimes circumstances are out of your control.

HAVE A SAFE BET

I have arms of my business that are so risky they're comparable to base-jumping. Other arms of my business are as safe and secure as a kiddie's bouncy castle (and just as fun). This contrast is important, as even disruptive start-ups should have one recurring revenue stream to rely on. Although as I've admitted, *The Collective* print magazine does not make a profit, I know that my books and speaking gigs bring in a regular, more than generous income and that they are just a handful of safe bets in place while the magazine finds its feet. For an entrepreneur this could be anything – a part-time job for those at the very beginning of their journey – a stopgap to ensure you always have a drip, drip of funds to quench your thirst.

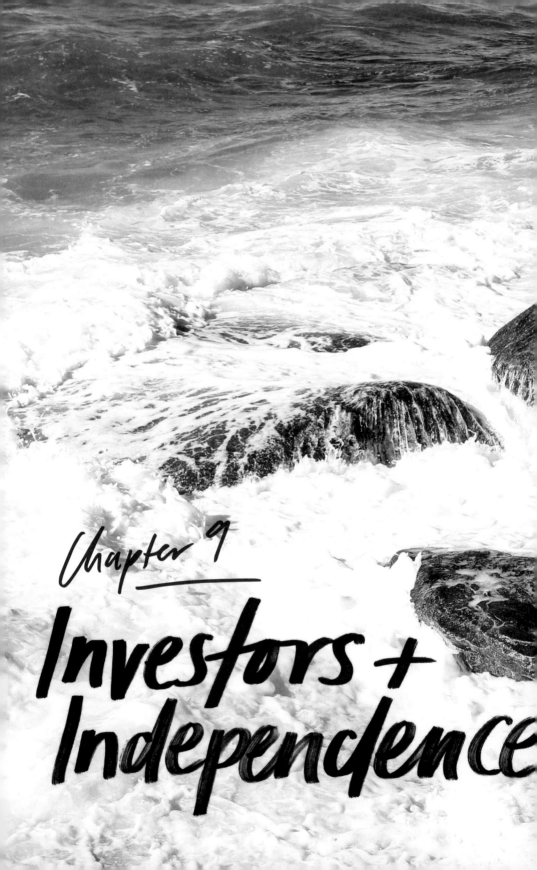

Chapter 9

Investors + Independence

have often been heard quoting the mantra: "You have as many hours in a day as Beyoncé." By that I mean that we're all capable of the same achievements, if we have the right attitude, if we're dedicated, determined, know how to adapt, react, twist and change to make the most of every opportunity. I know Beyoncé might not be the obvious business role model, but this isn't the only reason I relate to Queen B. To paraphrase the Destiny's Child song lyrics from back in the day, "The shoes on my feet I've bought it, the clothes I'm wearing I've bought it... I depend on me, I depend on me..." And yes I am singing and gyrating in my chair as I write this...

At this point you're probably thinking – has Lisa lost the plot? Well, I am nine chapters into writing a book, which means nine chapters of dawn writing, midnight brainstorming and nightmares that I accidentally delete the file with 100,000 of my words in it. I probably do have a few less marbles by now, BUT I stand by my Beyoncé reference as being appropriate. I am an independent businesswoman and I want to shout it from the rooftops. At the time of writing this chapter I own every single share of *The Collective*. I haven't had to take out a single bank loan, I don't owe any money against the business (although I do have several mortgages). I have been an entrepreneur for 14 years and don't have to repay anyone a single cent. Which is a very nice, and slightly surprising, position to be in.

Whenever I tell other entrepreneurs that I am the only investor in my company, many have the same reaction – surprise. Most people just think about traditional routes when finding investors – they simply can't understand how I have challenged, flipped and disrupted the norm to build something so big on the smell of an oily rag. That makes me laugh out loud, although I understand their confusion. I know that to many start-up founders, finding investors is the Holy Grail, the make or break, the sink or swim factor. So, why have I decided to actively avoid pursuing them up until this point? To be honest, I haven't needed them because of the strategies I've talked about in this book and more that I will go into in this chapter. Without meaning to sound boastful, I'm just very, very good at getting money through other means without having to give away any equity, out of desperation and a bit of creative and lateral thinking. This is why, for the first two years of *The Collective* I decided to go at it completely alone.

I do want to make one thing clear – I am not anti-investor. In fact, between you and me I am currently in 'talks'. There is a good chance that by the time I type the final full stop on this book, I will no longer be going it alone (more on that later, I promise). But, if and when I do choose to part with a portion of my brand's equity, I will have done it at my own pace, in my own way, on my own terms, at the right time for my brand, rather than because I had no other option. There are many pros and cons of independence versus investors, as owning 100 per cent of equity also means you shoulder 100 per cent of the risk, so I would never say that my way is the right way. I just hope to show there are different options, which can be equally abundant without having to relinquish too much control of your company. Most entrepreneurs are fiercely independent, with a stubborn streak, and don't really like to answer to others. Isn't this why we decided to go it alone, pursue our passions and chase a career without compromise in the first place?

"For me, making money is about freedom," says entrepreneur Jason Fried, the founder and CEO of the web design and software firm Basecamp (formerly known as 37Signals) and co-author of the best-selling book *Rework*. "When you owe people money, they own you – or at least they own your schedule." It might sound arrogant, but in the early stages of the magazine, I just didn't want anyone else slowing me down. As my amazing team will tell you (or warn you) I move at an extremely relentless, fast pace when it comes to making, changing and switching decisions, forever reacting and reassessing so that my brand evolves, improves and keeps one step ahead of other market leaders.

How would I move at this speed if I had multiple stakeholders to check in with and multiple opinions to consider? I've spoken to other magazine editors who have to wait for approval from five different people in five different countries to change the colour of one single full stop on a magazine masthead. Unless I moved my investors into my house, into my bedroom, how could I make the kind of lightning-bolt, middle-of-the-night decisions that have shaped our success? You know the kind where you sit bolt upright in bed and yell, "Game changer!" because suddenly everything becomes clear? At the early stages of my business, where every second counted and every decision could be fatal, I perhaps selfishly didn't want to have to explain, justify or get the thumbs up on my thought process. I wanted to move at my speed, in the direction of my inner compass.

When I started my marketing agency back in the day, we had a client who I loved dearly – probably a little too dearly, as at the time it was in danger of clouding my judgment. We used to produce a landed product for AU$6.50 a unit – now that included conceptualising, creative direction, producing the prototyping, creating the actual product, distribution, shipping, setting up photo shoots, styling, the list went on... The profit to us was quite literally 30 cents to 50 cents per unit, if that. They were then selling the product for AU$40 a unit. When you do the maths, at runs of 40,000 products a time, we were making a maximum of AU$20,000 for a whole massive heap of work, whereas they were making around AU$1,340,000 per run. Go figure.

The upside (or downside, depending on how you look at it) was I truly loved working with them. They were the kind of client who you genuinely love hanging out with, our meetings overran from lunch into the evening. But a little thing kept ticking away in my head going, "This is kind of madness, whichever way you string it. We're doing all the work and making a fraction of what they are bringing in overall..." And so I eventually decided to launch our own products, under our own name, so that we could reap the profits. My team had proved they had the knowledge to do so; it was time to step out from another brand's shadow in conjunction with *The Collective* to bolster our revenue and keep the print mag alive.

With that product line we effectively started by collaborating and then became independent when it suited us to do so. When we first started working for this client years earlier, if we had tried to produce an independent product line back then, we wouldn't have come close to selling 40,000 units because unlike the clients we were servicing, we didn't have a platform, a big profile or an adequate distribution funnel. At that point it was better for us to work for them because a part of a pie was better than no pie, and we would rather make 50 cents per unit than a big fat zero.

Here's my question to you, which will help you decide whether it's time to chase investors or to back yourself. Would you rather have 100 per cent of a $500,000 business or 51 per cent of a $50 million one? As I've said many times before, business is a dance and at different times, as you twirl around the ballroom, you might want to take the lead. At other times, you might be fine to stand on your partner's feet like a happy child and be whirled around in circles by someone who knows the steps better than you do. Both are fun. Both are liberating. Both might leave you flat on your arse with your skirt over your head. But whatever you decide, choose it for the right reasons – and realise there are more options than you probably imagine. Right now my vision is enormous and very global and so as I mentioned earlier, for the first time I am actually considering outside investment. I am not attached to owning the whole company at all. I just want the very best leverage to help me achieve what I have set out to do.

Anyone who lives within their means suffers from a lack of imagination.

—Oscar Wilde

HOLLER FOR DOLLARS

Historically, less than one per cent of start-up funding for US companies came from venture capital, with the rest divided between self-funding, loans, credit, family and friends and crowdfunding. See! There are other options. The secret is identifying your unique selling points, skill sets and shareable assets (and looking beyond the obvious).

It's easy to forget in this age of crowdfunding that entrepreneurs before digital profit-seeking platforms had to get off their backsides, get out from behind their computer screens and find creative, imaginative – and sometimes risky – ways to access cash flow to fund the early stages of their business. The founders of Airbnb sold their own brands of breakfast cereal to raise their initial funding (they were called Obama O's and Cap'n McCain – and no, I'm not kidding).

In the early stages of Google, when Larry Page needed to find US$15,000 to purchase a terabyte of storage space, he and co-founder Sergey Brin relied on the power of plastic, admitting, "We had to use all of our credit cards and our friends' credit cards and our parents' credit cards…" It could have backfired, clearly, but before the debt collectors came knocking, he and Sergey then raised US$100,000 in seed money from Andy Bechtolsheim, co-founder of Sun Microsystems. And the rest is history.

Every week I am lucky enough to meet a heap of kick-arse entrepreneurs and I am constantly amazed by the lengths that founders go to in the pursuit of funding and the imaginative, creative – and sometimes very risky – ways they have afforded to take the first step into the start-up scene. I've heard of founders renting out their couches to backpackers to pay for prototype development, of tech founders working part-time as science tutors, and even earning cash as nudey life-drawing models (at least you'll have an eye-catching portrait to hang in your office, when you can afford one).

I'll never forget one memorable story of two software developers from America who, to raise money for their medical software company Smart Medical Solutions, entered a competition to design and shoot a beer commercial. It was not at all in line with their start-up's mission, which was to create a software program to help oncologists track and administer patients' treatments, but they had their eye on the first prize – a one-week holiday to Jamaica for nine people. When they won, instead of going on the trip they asked the beer brand for the cash equivalent – US$20,000 – and they agreed.

I love stories like these because they remind me that there are many, many different ways to get what you want, and if you can scrape through the early days as an independent entrepreneur you'll be in a far stronger position to get investors later. Think about it this way; how much easier will it be to attract the best investors in the business if you already have a brand with clout rather than an unknown name, an untested idea and nothing concrete to show for your vision? If you can make it alone through those early days and prove your worth on your own, you'll be a far more attractive asset when you do put yourself out there. I truly do believe that riches favour the brave.

THE START-UP
COST CHECKLIST

- [ ] Domain name
- [ ] Internet connection and web hosting
- [ ] Website build
- [ ] SEO
- [ ] Branding and logo development
- [ ] Signage
- [ ] Workspace rental
- [ ] Workspace furniture and fit-out
- [ ] Phone installation and ongoing utility costs
- [ ] Legal set-up and ongoing costs
- [ ] Business registration
- [ ] Patents
- [ ] Trademarks
- [ ] License fees or permits
- [ ] Bookkeeping (in-house or consultancy)
- [ ] Accounting
- [ ] Business insurance
- [ ] In-house CFO or external consultancy
- [ ] Travel costs
- [ ] Staffing and recruitment costs
- [ ] Uniforms if applicable
- [ ] Stationery and office supplies
- [ ] Launch event/promotion
- [ ] Advertising
- [ ] Marketing
- [ ] Public relations
- [ ] Technology (laptops/software /cloud access)
- [ ] Cost of goods sold (prototype development, production, distribution)
- [ ] Hurt money (every start-up will have a few surprises so factor this in early)

Find peace with profit.

HIGH HOPES AND BIG PAY-OUTS

Here is a surprising truth that I've learned – it can be easier to get someone to part with $50,000 than $5000. And yes, I have got that the right way around. I'll give you a specific example related to *The Collective*, even though I appreciate you're probably not running a magazine, but most businesses are the same at the core, so look for the similarities rather than the differences.

In magazine land, most publications focus on selling advertising per page. For example, a fashion brand wants a one-page advert. That might be AU$8000. When we launched *The Collective* I identified a problem with this very early on in our dealings – boy, it was time-consuming! If we need to generate several million dollars a year just to break even, that's an awful lot of separate AU$8000 deals to strike, an awful lot of doors to knock on, an awful lot of clients to wine and dine.

So, I decided to think on my feet, despite the fact at that stage nobody in the industry knew anything about our new brand or cared about this self-proclaimed editor Lisa Messenger, who had zero experience in the industry. Rather than asking brands to part with AU$8000, I asked them for AU$50,000… per month… locked into a six-month contract. That meant I was asking them to commit to signing over AU$300,000. I have to admit I think this is where my naivety worked in my favour because I've since spoken to experienced magazine insiders who said they'd never have dared ask for that much, because they know that advertising budgets have been cut across all industries and they'd just expect the answer to be no. I didn't have that attitude. Oh, I knew I was asking for a lot, but I just had to make sure what I was offering in return was worth it.

The first thing I did was look at our saleable assets… then I broke them down… and then I broke them down further. This is something I recommend any start-up does, stripping back layers, fragmenting and then reforming in a new shape, a new structure. Okay, *The Collective* is a print magazine and so our content is our main currency, but when you slice that down further there are many ways we can offer an advertising brand exposure, and a single flat ad is only the beginning. There are opportunities for advertorials, for giveaways, competitions, to gift their product to our favourite reader's letter.

Then there are other tangible assets I've purposefully built off the back of the magazine, as I've mentioned before – do they want me to come in and do a motivational speech to their team? Could they have banners at a Collective Hub event or sample their products in our goodie bags? Do they want 5000 copies of my book to gift to their stakeholders at Christmas? The list really does go on and on...

Suddenly, rather than asking them to exchange AU$8000 for one flat-page asset, we are offering a AU$50,000-a-month multi-layered, highly engaging, long-running, over-arching package with plentiful touch points and opportunity for exposure. It is a far deeper, more trusting relationship, as we are offering access to our community, a highly engaged audience, and repetitive mentions over a six-month period. Also, because these types of deals are all about quality rather than quantity, it gave me the power to hand-pick the select brands I wanted to offer them to, ensuring their morals and ethics were in line with *The Collective* movement. Now, perhaps you can understand why I haven't borrowed money or had equity partners up to this point – why would I give away equity when I can go out and make deals worth AU$300,000 a nod? (NB you have to be prepared to commit – this takes a LOT of hard work).

I don't think anyone is very comfortable asking a third-party for money – especially entrepreneurs who are by nature usually ambitious, A-type personalities. We like to think of ourselves as invincibly self-sufficient. But if a deal is struck in the right way, with the right balance of power and a fair and even currency exchange, I don't think there's anything more empowering. It's all about learning to give with gusto – and take with grace.

CELEBRATE GOOD TIMES

In 2013, Drew Houston, the CEO of file-sharing site Dropbox, posted a screenshot of his online bank account on a blog, showing the moment he received a deposit from the company's first-ever funding round – an impressive credit of US$1.2 million from Sequoia Capital. Was this an overshare? Was it bragging? No, not at all (check out his caption with the screenshot: "At first, I was ecstatic – that number has two commas in it! I took a screenshot – but then I was sick to my stomach. Someday these guys are going to want this back. What the hell have I gotten myself into?"). Even if he was, why shouldn't the start-up founder be proud of such a magical money milestone? Why is it perfectly acceptable to post, pin, tweet and 'gram every other intimate moment of our lives – babies, engagements and even funerals – but not share evidence of a milestone moment such as this one?

To me, this screenshot isn't arrogant but inspiring – it should serve as an example to other entrepreneurs that anything is possible and the dogged and sometimes demoralising pursuit is worth it, that all the heads you see shake and doors that close in your face are instantly forgotten when a win does happen. This is why you keep pushing through all the "nos" – for the sheer overwhelming joy when you get one "yes". I'll never forget logging on to my online bank account a few months after that meeting with one of Australia's largest banks to see a deposit that seemed like a fortune to me. It wasn't about the money as much as what that figure symbolised. To me, that series of numbers felt like a passcode, which enabled me to crack open a lock and step through a door. A door that would lead into my new life, and an opportunity to enhance and inspire the lives of others.

But, while I do agree every founder who receives a windfall – whether through investment, venture capital, sponsorship or crowdfunding – should take time to stop, celebrate, punch the air and share the news with their community, it's also vitally important to keep it in perspective. I know $100,000 can seem like a fortune when you're running a business from your parents' garage (no shame in that – it's how Steve Jobs started) but the sad truth is, in this day and age, even six figures will not last for long when you're hell bent on expanding, scaling and world (or corner of the world) domination.

Recently, investors like Bill Gurley and Fred Wilson have voiced concern that venture capitalists are lending too much to high-risk projects. As entrepreneurs we shouldn't bank on the assumption that there will always be an endless supply of cash from investors. I have seen this happen – a start-up gets a big financial backer, pockets a lump sum of money and then in their excitement spends, spends, spends with no regard for long-term planning and future visioning. It's an easy mistake to make (I've already told you about my treadmill incident!).

So, keep pushing, thriving, driving and looking for the next opportunity, even before the balloons you hung to celebrate your first investment have deflated. Because while I am in no way addicted to money, I am totally, 100 per cent addicted to the thrill of watching my business expand far beyond my expectations (over and over again).

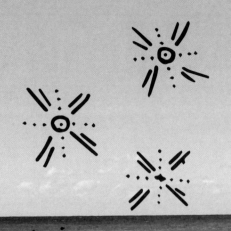

Dare to deserve.
You should know
your own worth.

10 WAYS TO RAISE MONEY

A GOVERNMENT GRANT

In many countries, governments offer grants to encourage innovative thinkers (in Australia search under business.gov.au for more information). Many of these grants only take applicants at certain times of the year so, to stay informed of the deadlines, set up a Google alert for "Start-up grant" so you never miss an announcement of a new program.

FRIENDS AND FAMILY

Many founders joke that the key to finding funding is in the 'three Fs' – friends, family and fools. The first two have certainly been known to support a lot of start-ups. However, if you are borrowing from loved ones treat it as an official business dealing just like any other. Get the advice of a lawyer or at the very least, put something in writing so there is a contract in place to rule out any confusion about repayment later.

PEER LENDING

Although the idea has been around for a while, 'P2P' lending has recently become a buzz phrase, where websites such as SocietyOne, RateSetter, DirectMoney and ThinCats match savers and borrowers using an algorithm, cutting out the middle man of a bank and in doing so offering competitive interest rates, because in theory they have less overheads than a bricks-and-mortar bank. The key here is to do your research and still seek advice from a financial advisor before signing.

CROWDFUNDING

The crowdfunding space is awash with people raising money for everything from prototype development to IVF treatment, so how do you stand out from the throngs? Instead of signing up to big names like Indiegogo, try a crowdfunding site specific to your niche industry. Pubslush, the crowdfunding site for authors, has a higher success rate for publishing than Kickstarter. There's also Seed&Spark offering crowdfunding for filmmakers and GiveForward for the medical treatments.

START AN ONLINE STALL

Marketplaces like Etsy offer a great way for start-ups to test a product, and also raise some funds to develop into a fully-fledged business. Just take note of the site's rules and regulations – for Etsy, everything sold must be handmade, vintage (defined as older than 20 years) or a craft supply. Alternatively, anyone can set up an eBay or Amazon marketplace but factor in shipping costs if offering sales worldwide.

ANGEL INVESTOR

Celebrities like Ashton Kutcher and Justin Timberlake have shone a light on angel investors, by using their movie millions to back start-up companies. But it's not only superstars who are sharing their wealth and their knowledge. Matchmaking sites like AngelList and Gust allow founders to create a profile that can be browsed by independent investors. Unlike crowdfunding, be aware this is an investment rather than a gift, and you will be expected to give away revenue.

LEAVE THE COUNTRY

Okay, it may sound drastic, but it's not unheard of for founders – especially of tech companies that can be run remotely – to move to a country with a cheaper cost of living while getting their business off the ground. On the plus side the stress of starting a company could be easier to handle from a beach in Peru where beer is only $2 a bottle. On the negative side, it's a long way to go for face-to-face business meetings.

BRIDGE YOUR INVOICES

One of the toughest struggles for start-ups is the pay-gap between invoicing and waiting for an amount to be paid by a client or customer. Now 'invoicing advancing' services offer to bridge the gap by fronting the money as soon as an invoice has been billed. One of the leading websites is Fundbox and allows business owners to sign up for a membership and access the service. Be aware there is a fee, estimated at between US$52 and US$72 per US$1000.

WORK WITH A RETIREE

I know an entrepreneur who believes the biggest untapped resource for start-up funding is former heads of industries. Think about it; there is a generation of experts who have reached retirement age but still have the drive, desire – and possibly the funding – to keep a finger on the pulse of a market. The hard part is finding them, but if you do you could earn yourself a lifetime of knowledge, as well as financial backing (remember the power of the grey pound!).

KEEP YOUR DAY JOB

I know it's not the sexiest answer, but sometimes it's necessary to be a part-time entrepreneur before you're able to ditch your corporate life and commit. Be transparent with your employer – they will know if you're spending work hours typing up your business plan – and you might be surprised by how much they support you. Is it possible to cut down to a four-day week or ask for flexi-hours to give you some freedom to explore your ideas? A good boss will (fingers crossed) admire your initiative.

HOW TO GET A BANK LOAN

Traditionally, entrepreneurs and banks have not been the best of friends. Banks are so risk-adverse and entrepreneurs are huge risk takers. I never needed a bank loan – luckily – but I know many start-up founders who have gone to a bank with their vision and been met with an expression of disbelief. So, how do you win over a conventional bank manager with innovative thinking? Here's what I've gleaned from friends, experts and co-entrepreneurs who have walked this journey, which may help you.

Pre-pitch your pitch. It can be worth emailing the bank manager you're due to meet a brief written summary of your plan before you sit down face-to-face. This means they have time to do some research and, hopefully, can give you a "yes" or "no" on the spot. Once you're out of the room, out of sight and out of mind, the decision is less in your control.

Don't confuse your bank manager with a customer. I've met entrepreneurs who say the mistake they made was pitching to sell a product rather than getting the means to produce one. A bank manager wants to hear back-end details – facts, figures and a projected forecast – not a sales pitch on how your product or service can help them directly. Should you bring samples? Only if you're pitching a never-before-seen prototype.

Present your personal credit history. It might not seem relevant to share how you paid off your student loan and saved up for your first house deposit but, especially if your business doesn't have an established operating history, banks look at the founder's personal credit history for clues to their attitude to borrowing, spending and lending. Be transparent and produce all the information you can.

Research the bank's ethos. Do some ground work into recent initiatives the bank has supported, specifically any glory projects they've recently sent out press releases about. For instance, has a bank put a push on supporting environmental initiatives and if so, how could your start-up fall into that category? It's worth memorising the bank's mission statement and vision and dropping in key words to show you're on the same page.

Know your limits. Even with a small business loan, a bank will often require you to put up equity on your house as security. Don't get caught out if this topic comes up. If you jointly own your property, have a conversation with your partner before the meeting so you know whether this is a goer, and get independent advice from a financial advisor or accountant so you understand the implications.

Ask about add-ons. Show interest in the bank's products aimed at business owners. Many banks now offer small business savings accounts and credit cards especially for start-up founders. You don't need to sign up – and don't allow yourself to feel obligated to do so – but enquiring about these services shows that you're willing and represents a long-term customer. It also shows your long-term plan is to save as well as spend.

Don't arrive defeated. If you google advice on how to get a bank loan, many available blogs and articles are doom-laden takes of how it's almost impossible to get backing. Yet there are many success stories proving that it is perfectly do-able, so don't let naysayers deter you. When you do get a "yes" to a face-to-face meeting, arrive with the right attitude. You are doing them a favour by allowing them to be part of your journey. And remember – they wouldn't have agreed to meet you if funding start-ups wasn't in their jurisdiction.

only your mind controls your bottom line .

Chapter 10

Generosity

E ven at my lowest, brokest (if that is a word!) point, I still felt it was my duty to give something back to others.

When my book publishing business was at its peak, we donated over AU$2.4 million worth of books (measured by the RRP) in one single year to charities. One afternoon I sat down, added it up and couldn't believe it. I had literally given away an entire library. For nothing! At the time, if any charity came to us and asked for books to give away at their next event, to put in goodie bags or offer as part of an auction, I told my team to just say "yes" to everyone, because I firmly believe you get what you give, and what goes around comes around. (Also let's be honest, it raises the profile of our authors. I would be fibbing if I didn't admit that as a factor and part of a long-term win-win strategy.)

Let me first start this chapter by making a promise – I am not about to tell you to empty your pockets, rather, how to build giving into your business plan so it can benefit both parties. Because although I believe whole-heartedly that generosity matters and we all need to share and share alike to make the world go round, I am also at my core an entrepreneur with my feet grounded in reality. When it comes to generosity, I believe that both charities and individuals need to be far smarter about how they give and take. The reality is, if you are generous without boundaries, if your charitable acts aren't calculated and if you drain your well of resources, then in the long-term you won't be able to help anyone, because your business model will be a car crash. And it's hard to be both a victim and a saviour.

So, let's talk about giving versus over-attachment. I was recently at the third birthday party of one of my dear friends' children, and there seemed to be one buzz-phrase that I heard pop out of at least a dozen mums' mouths as they applauded their children. "Good sharing." Little Benny passes his toy car to another kid. "Good sharing." A pig-tailed little girl takes a piece of half-chewed banana from her mouth and puts in into her sister's mouth. "Good sharing." The social etiquette is deeply conditioned into us from the earliest age – if we share, we will be praised, if we share, we will be rewarded.

Which is a good thing, right? But, the bad side of this conditioning is that somewhere along the way I think sharing can become a duty – something we do because it is expected, because we'll be respected, so we'll be applauded – rather than something that we do because it boosts our personal harmony. We forget there are many benefits to giving, aside from a round of applause (giving has been shown to reduce blood pressure, lower stress levels, improve motivation and, not surprisingly, boost happiness). And so as soon as nobody is watching, we 'forget' to share our money and our knowledge, and we scoff down the last hot chip before our friend gets back from the bathroom. I overheard a girl in a coffee shop queue say recently, "Sh*t, I forget to check in on Facebook at the gym, I may as well not have done a workout." (Yes, really). I think the same can apply to generosity – if it isn't a public display, if our 'just giving' donation isn't tweeted, reposted and liked by those who know us, does it lose its value? Do we see the benefits? If a tree falls in a forest…

A study by the Australian National University has found that we, as a nation, are giving less to non-government organisations working in international development than ever (nine cents in every AU$100 in 2012/2013, down from 14 cents in every AU$100 in 2004). With a guilty twinge, we skip the online 'Add a donation' button when we're booking our plane tickets, we brush aside the street collectors because everyone knows they're just annoying, right? We have a blind spot for the donation boxes at checkouts because do they even really get emptied? We have a hundred different excuses to ignore a hundred different ways of sharing. But I really, truly do believe that you have to give to receive, whether it's actions, words or wealth. I believe that everyone has a basket of favours – you might give out 10 and then you have one favour left in the basket you can use yourself. It might sound a bit woo-woo but by that rule of thumb, because I gave out AU$2.4 million worth of books, I will have received AU$240,000 back in return. When I think of all the deals I've made, all the 'yeses' I've received from people who don't know me but believe in me and have backed me, then my faith in the power of reciprocity is restored. To receive wealth, happiness, love and contentment, you have to send it out into the world.

If you're a start-up founder thinking, "But, I'm barely surviving, I don't have anything spare to give," then I'm not going to tell you just to empty your pockets, as my charitable giving is still practical and pragmatic. Let's brush aside the warm fuzzy feeling of giving for a moment and really think – what do you actually have to offer? How can you build generosity into your business plan?

This is why I admire high-profile 'celebrity' (for want of a better word) givers who build a profile first and then use their platform to support a cause that matters to them. When it was revealed Jamie Oliver was paid £1.2 million per year to be the face of the UK supermarket brand Sainsbury's, the fee was criticised by the media for being ridiculously high. Yet, he used his position to make positive changes, with campaigns encouraging supermarket shoppers to switch to sustainable fish, and encouraging Sainsbury's to stop selling battery-farmed chickens. Jamie also passes his knowledge down to the next generation. In 2014, Jamie's Ministry of Food centres held more than 160 eight-week cooking courses and more than 150 workshops across the UK, teaching people how to cook with wholesome ingredients. Plus, roughly 150 apprentices have graduated from their apprenticeship programme since it began in 2002. Jamie – I'm a big fan of both you and your business model! Whether you can give $5 or $5 billion, my point is that you can – and should – build generosity into your business plan. Even if this means starting small and allowing your generosity to scale as your brand does. Make generosity part of your growth strategy and reap the rewards. As Winston Churchill said, "What is the use of living, if it be not to strive for noble causes and to make this muddled world a better place for those who will live in it after we are gone?"

'on't be trapped in
a poor mindset.

Count your blessings.
Be grateful.

ARE YOU AN OVERGIVER?

Ten years ago when I wrote my first book *Happiness Is…* I decided to give away a percentage of the profits to the charity Kids Helpline, despite the fact that at the time I was living hand-to-mouth and money certainly wasn't in abundance. I know, I know, I've spent this entire chapter talking about not giving beyond your means but I'm not being a hypocrite because that decision was extremely considered and in line with my personal purpose during that period. Just as I do at every big milestone in my life, before I made the decision I checked in with my 'why' and asked – why have I written this book, what is my end goal and what do I need to achieve for the project to feel fulfilling? Money didn't come into any of those answers, so I decided to donate it to a better cause. And the universe rewarded me hundreds of times over.

I wrote *Happiness Is…* at the lowest, darkest point in my life in the hope that interviewing other people about what made them happy would turn into a personal experiment to pull me out of the gutter. I didn't write it to raise my profile, to make myself a millionaire or to end up on *Oprah*, but in the simple hope that by meeting happy people, their contentment would be contagious – and it was. Just writing the book was the most wonderful, cathartic journey of self-development, and the emotional boost it gave me was a priceless reward in itself.

Fast-forward a decade to shortly after the launch of *The Collective*. I remember being at a networking event and the head of a not-for-profit asked me, "So, what charity are you going to align the magazine with?" Her eyebrows shot up in surprise when I boldly replied, "None." Not at that moment anyway. At that time, I believed *The Collective* was still too young, too new and too vulnerable to commit to one, single organisation for a number of reasons. Firstly, our revenue stream at that stage wasn't stable, so I didn't yet know what level of financial long-term donation I could commit too. It also didn't serve our readers because in every issue of the magazine we profile four or five amazing organisations across the world, who are changing the lives of many people in many different ways. I wanted to continue to share as many good causes as possible with our readers, going broader rather than deeper, which is why I saw aligning with one charity, at that stage, as counter-productive. My point around this was that rather than attaching to and going deep with one charity early on, my real mission is about touching the lives of hundreds of thousands of people, which has now turned into touching the lives of millions. *The Collective* in a way is my cause, and our mandate is to inspire as many people as humanly possible. And so every story very purposefully is authentic, raw and real, is attainable and relatable rather than unreachable, and therefore people have the power to believe in their own dreams. We have hundreds upon hundreds of thousands of letters saying how much our stories have changed people's lives or propelled them into action or given them the impetus to change course. We also ensure that within our stories we give a hearty weighting to showcasing a number of charities and not-for-profits and social cause-related projects from around the globe. So, no, at this point, why would I focus on one particular charity or cause when we can touch so many? Of course, in our work we come across particular ones that resonate strongly with the team, and in those instances we may go a little deeper in our giving or our contribution of time or resources to help them on their journey or give them further share of voice.

One person I have massive respect for when it comes to generosity is Bill Gates – who, along with his wife Melinda, has pledged to give away 95 per cent of their fortune to charity rather than leave it to his children. It's an amazing decision and yet I love that he made it from a cool, business mindset. "I'm certainly well taken care of in terms of food and clothing," explains Bill, "Money has no utility to me beyond a certain point. Its utility is entirely in building an organisation and getting the resources out to the poorest in the world." The technology magnate isn't just walking into the middle of the street and throwing his money into the air, he has put systems, processes and measured resources in place to share his wealth in a way that he thinks can make a real difference, after calculating exactly what he and his family need to live.

And he's not the only business-minded giver. Bill and Melinda Gates launched The Giving Pledge in 2010, where they began asking the wealthiest people in the world (it is focused on billionaires) to commit to giving more than half of their wealth "to philanthropy or charitable causes either during their lifetime or in their will". When new billionaires sign up they each write a "giving pledge" to explain their decision to give away the majority of their fortune, when they plan to do so and how they plan to do it. I find these pledges fascinating, not just because I am blown away by each person's generosity, but also because each giver's pledge is still steeped in entrepreneurialism. They are considered, calculated and proactive, combining a big heart with business savvy. Many freely admit they're not ready to give away their wealth – yet – because they still need it to expand and scale their empires and fulfil their personal purpose first. Is there anything wrong with this? I don't think so! In fact, I think responsible givers do so while protecting their own purpose. Although this might sound a little woo-woo, the self-help writer Stephen Richards writes, "The law of sacrifice postulates that we need to give in order to receive... Cosmic Ordering says, receive before you give." If that is a little hippie for your liking, then just think of it this way – how will you continue to give long-term if you have nothing left to sustain yourself?

In an amazing article the author Elizabeth Gilbert wrote for Oprah's website, she speaks about the difference between generosity and "overgiving", and how after the success of *Eat, Pray, Love* she fell into the trap of the latter. "I went on a full-octane overgiving bender," she explains, "I gave to some charities and good causes, but mostly I gave heaps of money to people I knew and loved. I paid off my friends' credit card bills, caught them up on their mortgages, financed their dream projects, bought them plane tickets, tuition, therapy, gym memberships, vehicles. Sometimes (well, twice), I even bought them houses."

The turning point came when Elizabeth realised she was giving with the wrong agenda. "Now, overgiving is not quite the same thing as generosity," she explains. "Generosity is neither entangling nor aggressive, because the generous person doesn't expect anything in return. The overgiver doesn't expect anything in return either – except to be petted and feted and praised and loved unconditionally for the rest of time." Years earlier, she met a monk in India who had warned her, "Never give anyone more than they are emotionally capable of receiving, or they will have no choice but to hate you for it."

This is what I try to remember when it comes to *The Collective* and supporting good causes. Although I wish I could help everyone (really and truly), at this point in my life, in my business, I only have so much I can sustainably give away. But that shouldn't make me scared of giving away anything. I don't think that business and philanthropy are mutually exclusive, I think you can act from your heart and your head at the same time, and manage to both help others while protecting yourself, your vision and your future. So, do give. Generously. But, don't give more than you can afford to, don't give so much it leaves you in turmoil, don't give with such abandon that it leaves you resentful, drained and unable to continue. I will always believe that what you give, you get, but my karmic credit card does have a limit. If by sharing my light with the world it leaves me in the red, then I won't be able to help anyone in the long run.

We lose ourselves in the
things we love, we
find ourselves there too

—Kristin Martz

Bill and Melinda Gates' Giving Gang

SARA BLAKELY

"At this stage in my life most of my time remains dedicated to growing the business. My hope is that my continued investment in Spanx will pay even greater dividends to help women. I have been setting aside profits since the start of Spanx with the goal that when the time comes I will have an amazing opportunity to help women in an even bigger way... Setting aside the money in my foundation is only part of the preparation, learning the most effective way to give is the other."

GEORGE LUCAS AND MELLODY HOBSON

"My pledge is to the process; as long as I have the resources at my disposal, I will seek to raise the bar for future generations of students of all ages. I am dedicating the majority of my wealth to improving education."

BILL AND KAREN ACKMAN

"My earliest memories include my father's exhortations about how important it is to give back. These early teachings were ingrained in me, and a portion of the first dollars I earned, I gave away. Over the years, the emotional and psychological returns I have earned from charitable giving have been enormous. The more I do for others, the happier I am."

RICHARD AND JOAN BRANSON

"As and when we take monies out of the Virgin Group of companies the majority of it will be invested in entrepreneurial approaches to help make a difference in the world. We want the value created by the Virgin Group to be used to invest in new collaborative approaches to addressing issues, where business, governments and not-for-profits join forces to create a healthy, equitable and peaceful world for future generations to enjoy."

ANDREW AND NICOLA FORREST

"... while giving responsibly is challenging to do well, you will find it even more satisfying than the exhilaration you experienced when creating your enterprises. It was your logic, intuition, focus, foresight, good fortune, relentless determination and work capacity that produced the wealth you now ponder the future of. Yet it is also these same powerful talents that cause you to ask yourself, could I became a major philanthropist and responsibly use my wealth to improve communities and the lives of those less fortunate, potentially touching millions of people?"

TAD TAUBE

"There has existed in the minds of refugees who have been embraced by this great country, a level of gratitude for the opportunities [made] available to us that is somewhat analogous to a debt that we feel needs to be repaid. Some of us refer to that feeling as wanting to 'give back' – I personally prefer to call it wanting to 'share opportunity'."

HOW TO BE GENEROUS WHEN YOU HAVE NOTHING TO GIVE

But, of course, we're not all blessed with billions – whether it's inherited or earned over many years of hard work like the incredible pledgers previously mentioned – but take heart, when you're in the start-up phase you can be generous with more than just cash.

WITH YOUR WORDS

The day before writing this chapter, I posted a photo of the front cover of *GQ* magazine on my Instagram page. Immediately someone responded, "Why on earth would you share a competitor's magazine cover?" to which I laughed out loud. I shared it because it was a stunning cover with the amazing Chris Hemsworth and I wanted to give a big shout-out and kudos to my colleague Nick Smith at *GQ* for starters. People (in any industry) tend to stay in their patch and guard it with their lives, setting the competitor up as the enemy. But why shouldn't we applaud each other?

WITH RECIPROCITY

I am a big believer in reciprocity and abundance, because I believe there is enough work/wealth/happiness to go around for everyone. This is the reason I put an advertisement for the wedding magazine *White* in the pages of *The Collective*, and didn't ask them to pay for it. The mag's editor Carla Burrell has been equally supportive of us, coming to events and workshops I have run. In response, they ran an advertisement for my last book *Life & Love*. Share the love, I say. Value exchange is everything. I recently gave a couple of complimentary ads away to Animals Australia, as it's something I'm personally really passionate about.

WITH PHILANTHROPY

I love this phrase, started by a US group called The Secret Society for Creative Philanthropy, who go around the city carrying out $100 good deeds, from giving 'mini-grants' to struggling artists, buying desserts for strangers and even scattering coins across primary school playgrounds for kids to find. I'd squeeze this even further and say you can share a lot of love for $10 too.

WITH YOUR SPACE

Do you have a spare desk in your office? Why not offer it to a freelancer who needs to escape the solitude of their apartment? This doesn't have to just mean a business space – are you using your parking space or could you lend it to a neighbour to use when their grandparents come to visit? Can you offer your friend a corner of your garage to store her worldly possessions when she's in between houses? Look around you and see what you have to offer.

WITH YOUR TIME

Don't have a day to spare to help others? How about 10 minutes? The micro-volunteering website Skills For Change allows good-hearted people with useful skill sets (logo design, copyrighting, publicity) to complete simple tasks for not-for-profit organisations, and all the small jobs are able to be completed remotely, so you don't even need to leave your office to do your bit.

WITH YOUR PROMISES

Okay, we might not all end up being billionaires, but we can still learn a lot from the Gates' idea, especially when it comes to forecasting philanthropy. You might not have the excess funds now but make your own pledge to give a certain amount to a certain charity once you make over a certain amount of money. Be specific, write it down, stick it up somewhere public and don't let yourself forget it.

Chapter 11

Should Money Change You?

recently went out for a meal with two of my dearest friends, who for the sake of anonymity we'll call Anna and James (you'll understand why I'm not using their real names in a minute!). Anna and James are two of the most successful, generous and grounded people I know (a rare combination) and so I have to admit my jaw dropped when James told me a story about a mistake that he made (and 'mistake' is an understatement). He had recently flown a highly-regarded trend spotter to Australia from America, to discuss collaborating on a project that James was planning. To convince this trend spotter to consider it, James had offered to fly him here, put him up in a hotel and cover his expenses… unfortunately he made the mistake of not clarifying exactly what that meant. So, the guy arrived, stayed for four nights at a very trendy hotel in Melbourne, they talked, they agreed to collaborate, it all went very well…. until a week later James received his invoice for expenses. And it was US$34,000. What the…?
It turns out this trend spotter's definition of 'expenses' was a little more than three meals a day and the odd snack from a mini bar. Apparently, when he travels he doesn't bring a suitcase, and instead buys new outfits when he lands at his destination (we're talking an Armani suit here!). On top of this, he expensed US$900 worth of spa treatments, and a bottle of aged whiskey he had sent to his room that cost US$9000.

My jaw dropped when I heard the story – so did James pay it? Yes! He felt it was his fault and oversight for not specifying exactly what 'expenses' meant and placing a cap on the maximum that he'd pay. "Plus, the project we're collaborating on will make me triple that amount back in the end," he argues, "Although it did make me sick to have to pay that, in the long-run the relationship will be worth it."

Why am I telling you this? I'm sure that everyone who reads this story will have a slightly different reaction. You might think it represents grotesque excess and all that is wrong with consumerism. Maybe you're mentally calculating that invoice is more than a year's salary for some people. Or perhaps you feel inspired, imagining yourself in the position where you could comfortably spend US$34,000 and laugh about it (through gritted teeth) a few weeks later. As for me, I wasn't exactly sure how I felt when I heard the story – perhaps a mixture of all of the above if I'm honest. But what really intrigued me is how James could be so calm about such a financial f**k up, when he is an entrepreneur who sees life as a series of spreadsheets. "Oh, it was awful," admits James. To look on the bright side (as I always try to do) you could argue that client probably had the time of their life and so it will have improved their business relationship and heightened James' chances of making similarly fruitful deals with them in the future.

I found it interesting that James was able to deal with the guilt of his mistake by taking a step back, seeing the big picture and allowing himself to realise that at that point in his life and in his business, he could afford to take that hit, rather than torturing himself with how stupid he'd been. Whether or not you ethically agree that any bottle of whiskey is worth that much money is irrelevant, because from a purely business perspective James could afford to take the hit.

A few days after I met up with James and Anna I did a speaking gig at a health retreat, where I met a lovely entrepreneur who had just launched her own jewellery business. During our chat, she told me she was struggling with money as she'd recently had to pay AU$300 to get some business cards printed. She spoke about that AU$300 loss in the same way as James discussed his US$34,000 expense bill, although to many of us the two amounts are at totally different ends of the spectrum. But to both those entrepreneurs, their respective pay-outs caused the same amount of hurt in comparison to their revenue stream. To an early-stage founder of a bedroom start-up AU$300 was worth mentioning, although I bet James would see that as pocket money.

I am not relaying or comparing these stories to say that one is right and one is wrong, or to judge people at either end of the spectrum, but to try and show that all wealth is relative and as your bank balance grows, and your brand builds and your disposable income increases, it is important to shift your perspective, to constantly check your reality and to move your goalposts. As we come to the final chapter in this book, hopefully you're one step closer to riches (whatever that means to you) and so the question is – what next? I want you to be aware of the future ramifications, and tackle a big question that is relevant to the above story – should money change you?

Oh, I know the expected, socially acceptable answer to this big question is, "No, of course not". We are taught that even if we come into money, we must stay true to our roots, remember where we came from and not allow it to change our behaviour. But does this really serve us? Will it allow us to grow and live life as our truest, fullest versions? Or is it an offshoot of the 'money is evil' mindset that I hope to have erased in you? Don't get me wrong, when it comes to our values, ethics and intimate relationships I do not think money should change you on a heart level. But when it comes to business, it might surprise you to hear that I think money should change you. In fact, I believe that it's imperative. Otherwise, what's the point of making money in the first place?

I'm not saying that I ever, ever, EVER purposefully pay AU$1000 for a single dinner, but I am at a point in my journey where, after a LOT of hard work, I could pay that bill if it came to it, without having to wash the dishes in the restaurant. And, I think it's important as an entrepreneur-on-the-up to stop and let yourself realise that, to adjust your expectations and actions appropriately. If I was still making business decisions from the mindset of the Lisa who earned AU$10 an hour working at a fried chicken shop (I was fired BTW), or Lisa who earned AU$25,000 a year working at an estate agent, then I would be doing a disservice to the brand that I've worked so hard to build, and my personal motto that every person should live life as the fullest version of themselves.

So, allow money to drive you but not guide you, allow it to fuel your mission but not shift your ethos. Media entrepreneur Tim O'Reilly puts it so aptly, "Money is like gasoline during a road trip. You don't want to run out of gas on your trip, but you're not doing a tour of gas stations."

USE IT OR LOSE IT

I often think of a friend's grandmother who for her 20th birthday was given AU$100 worth of shares by her then-employer, and for her entire life refused to touch them. When she died well into her nineties, those shares were worth over AU$1.5 million. Yet, some few years before her death, when she was in perfect health, she refused to fly two hours to her granddaughter's wedding (a AU$250 flight) because she said she couldn't afford it, and she refused to allow anyone else to pay for it. Despite having an untouched fortune, she missed out on one of the most special moments of her granddaughter's life, because she hadn't allowed money to move her goalposts and was trapped in a mindset of scarcity. So, you can see my point when I say you should let money change, assist and elevate you.

Of course, there is a fine line between appreciation and arrogance, being go-getting and greedy, changing in the right way and the wrong way. In a TED interview, Bill and Melinda Gates speak about their children's inheritance and why they chose to give the majority of their wealth to charity rather than passing it down the bloodline. "We want to strike a balance," says Bill, "Where they have the freedom to do anything, but not a lot of money showered on them so they could go out and do nothing." To me, this is a sentiment all of us could learn from, whether we're entrepreneurs, employees, stay-at-home parents or teenagers.

I think the key to letting money change you – the right way – is allowing it to fuel your passion, expand your vision and help you get closer to your end goal, while not letting it shift your ethics, morals or values.

I watched a documentary once about the late American rapper Tupac '2Pac' Shakur, who sold over 75 million records. The documentary showed a clip of a very young Tupac talking about how offended he was after recently hearing someone refer to a woman as a bitch, and how rude he thought it was. He came across as so virtuous, biblical and clean-living, that it seemed impossible just a few years later, after fame and fortune hit, that he had transformed into a bling-covered mega-star whose lyrics were peppered with swear words. But, it seems proof of how much money – fast cars, women and being surrounded by 'yes' people – can shift our morals if we let it.

I was pondering this recently in a taxi on the way to a speaking gig in Melbourne. It was my third speaking gig in a week, which meant that over the course of three days I'd just earned about AU$30,000, with absolutely no physical outgoings except for my time because all my expenses had also been covered. It crossed my mind that if I was to sell *The Collective* and become a full-time public speaker, which my profile would now allow me to do, then I would probably make an awful lot more as a solo-preneur than I do running the business. Not to mention work less hours. But it has no interest to me right now because my 'why' is very clear – to use the platform of *The Collective* to produce inspiring content and build a community – rather than raise my profile as a solo-preneur. I don't need to be rich; I just want to reach people, inspire them and help them to see their potential and be the best version of themselves.

I often say I'm like Teflon when it comes to money, aware that it comes in and out, matter-of-fact about the freedom and choice it allows me, but never attached, never clinging, never sticking. On the extreme and tragic end of the scale, I once attended a course with a lovely guy who committed suicide two weeks later because he was convinced that he was in terrible, dire straights that he couldn't recover from, even though he'd shared in our group sessions that he was just AU$300,000 in debt. I'd heard his business plan; it seemed recoverable. What a sad loss that could have been avoided. It is so important to realise the power of money, that it can buy you influence and reach, but not to get too embroiled in it and the material side.

I love the quote from the late Polish journalist Ryszard Kapuściński who says, "Money changes all the iron rules into rubber bands." To me, this sums up how money should change you when it comes to your business actions. You should allow money to stretch you, and allow you to reach more people, without breaking you, stiffening or hardening your core. Money is the financial fuel for my machine, the oil on my Slip 'N Slide, which will allow me to move faster and bring you all along for the ride.

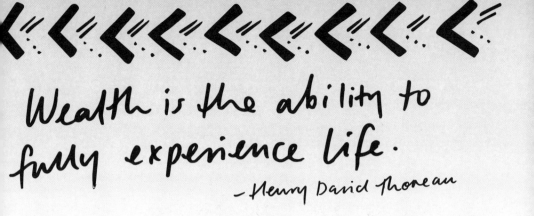

Wealth is the ability to fully experience life.

– Henry David Thoreau

FEELING GUILTY
(FOR NO GOOD REASON)

In his book *Revolution*, the British comedian Russell Brand writes, "Anyone who's been poor and gets rich is stalked by guilt and fear. Guilt because you know it isn't fair, that life hasn't changed for everyone, and fear because you feel like a fraud, that one day there'll be a knock on the door or a tap on the shoulder or a smack in the mouth and they'll take it back."

I am constantly amazed, surprised and, I admit, a little bit guilty that I find myself in such a prosperous position. Yet, I don't think this is necessarily a bad thing because it keeps me on my toes, reminds me of the transience of money and the fact that, as quickly as you can make it, you can also lose it. And that's okay too.

I wish I could say that reading this book will save you from ever making a mistake when it comes to money, but none of us is invincible, nor perfect. Failing fast and using downtimes as a learning curve are all part of being a daring and disruptive entrepreneur (as long as you don't purposefully hurt anyone else in the process). The truth is I still make mistakes, every single day. But, the difference is that now, rather than beating myself up, feeling frustrated and begrudging, as I would have done in the past, I look at my mistakes without attachment or resentment.

One of the triggers for writing this book was a particularly troublesome 48 hours near *The Collective*'s second birthday. I was hit by a series of financial blows in short succession, which although I can't go into them here, did cost me tens of thousands of dollars. I sat in my office looking at three emails asking for three overbearingly large figures. I had a choice for all three – to fight or pay even though I knew I wasn't in the wrong for any. It might surprise you to hear that I opted for the latter. Was I being a pushover? No, I was taking control of my situation and in this instance decided the short-term pay-out would hurt, but was better than the long-term, energetic struggle. And so I let it go... (I didn't end up having to pay two out of the three of these outgoings. It's funny how sometimes when you stop clinging to something so tightly it turns out your way.)

I want to leave you with an anecdote that represents my attitude to money. I hope this memory and lesson will stay with me whether I am a millionaire, become a billionaire or decide to retire to a hut on Necker Island and live among Richard Branson's flamingos.

A few years before launching *The Collective* I invested in another business – AU$50,000 – which was a huge amount of money to me at the time and involved pulling money from an ever-increasing mortgage to do so. These days, I would never, EVER get involved in such a business opportunity, as I hadn't done my due diligence, I was acting from a place of 'like' because I believed in the guy behind the business as an individual. I was buying into him without thinking logically... and I lost every cent of my investment. During the six years since then I've struggled with this mistake, blaming me, blaming him, blaming a set of circumstances for bringing us together.

But the weekend before I sat down to write this final chapter, backstage at a television studio waiting to go on to talk about *The Collective*, I suddenly, in a single instant, was able to reframe the situation in my mind and see details that I'd been ignoring because of my resentment. You see, that start-up founder who I invested in was the first person to believe in me on my early journey of self-discovery. He was the first stepping-stone in a series that turned my life around and enabled me to go on to find myself, my purpose and my passion. Yes, I lost AU$50,000 by investing in his company and believing in him. But he saved my life by investing and believing in me. So, as we reach the final page, I wish you all a life of abundance. An abundance of wealth, health, happiness, prosperity, peace and love, which should all feed into each other. Remember that money makes the world go around, but only passion, love, friendships and laughter turn it into a carousel...

ABOUT THE AUTHOR

Lisa Messenger is the vibrant, game-changing founder and editor-in-chief of *The Collective* as well as CEO of publishing house The Messenger Group. *The Collective* is an entrepreneurial lifestyle magazine distributed into over 37 countries with a mandate to disrupt, challenge and inspire. In addition, she has worked globally in events, sponsorship, marketing, PR and publishing.

Lisa has authored and co-authored over a dozen books and become an authority in the start-up scene, charting her rollercoaster ride to success in best-selling book *Daring & Disruptive: Unleashing the Entrepreneur* and its sequel *Life & Love: Creating the Dream*, which reached #1 on Booktopia. With fans including Sir Richard Branson, *New York Times* best-selling author Bradley Trevor Greive, Lisa's vision is to build a community of like-minded people who want to change the world.

Her passion is to challenge individuals and corporations to change the way they think, take them out of their comfort zone and prove that there is more than one way to do anything. She encourages entrepreneurial spirit, creativity and innovation and lives life to the absolute max. Most mornings she wakes up and pinches herself as to how incredible her life is, but is also acutely aware and honest about life's bumps and tumbles along the way.

She has a fascination for continual growth and in between being a serial entrepreneur and avid traveller, she spends most of her time in Sydney with her beautiful dog, Benny.

   @lisamessenger
#moneyandmindfulness

SPEAKING OPPORTUNITIES

Lisa is available for speaking opportunities. Her key message is "anything's possible".

Her presentation is highly engaging, active, motivational and really gets people wanting to jump out of their seats and take on the world!

Lisa uses a lot of tools, anecdotes, stories, how-to's and self-deprecating humour to take her audience on the journey.

Some of Lisa's favourite topics to speak on are:
- Cultivating a killer self-belief
- Finding passion and purpose
- Creating an amazing team culture
- Failing fast
- Strategic partnerships
- Thinking big and going global
- Challenging your personal limits and overall thinking
- Building a personal brand or business
- Disrupting in business and within a corporate
- Developing a sixth sense
- Investing in yourself

For more information, bookings, and bulk book sales enquiries, email pr@collectivehub.com or phone +61 2 9699 7216

"Lisa has had a long affiliation with the Australian Businesswomen's Network and has formed part of our Advisory Board. She chaired International Women's Day for the ABN and her passion, energy and dedication were an inspiration to all who she came in contact with."
SUZI DAFNIS – NATIONAL GENERAL MANAGER, AUSTRALIAN BUSINESSWOMEN'S NETWORK

"Lisa is the perfect example of what can be achieved by getting out there and having a go. Her 'never say die' attitude works wonders for anyone looking for that head start on the road to success."
BEN FORDHAM – JOURNALIST, CHANNEL NINE

Lisa is truly inspirational. Her energy is infectious and her story truly remarkable.
GARY PERLSTEIN – DIRECTOR, SPECIALTY FASHION GROUP

"Our appreciation and sincere thanks to you for your energy and inspiration that you shared with us last month. It was such a delight to have you participate in the Melbourne Fashion Festival Business Events. Hope to be in contact with you over time in the future as a part of the MFF Alumni community."
FELICITY BATH AND GRAEME LEWSEY – VAMFF

"Lisa Messenger was our keynote speaker recently at our annual Sydney Red Frogs Gala event. She was totally engaging with the audience; completely intuitive and on board with our strategies for the evening; extremely generous with her time; and was wonderfully approachable for our guests to have photographs etc. We would definitely recommend Lisa as a speaker."
CLAUDINE ALAME – NSW CO-ORDINATOR, RED FROGS

"Lisa was recommend to me as an absolute dynamo entrepreneur, who was passionate about people and the world we live in. To say that was an understatement doesn't do it justice. We were so blown away by Lisa's energy and chutzpah to make things happen, we invited her to speak at our event two years in a row. Yes she is brave, and yes she is an inspirational entrepreneur and great speaker. But what I, and our audience, connected with, was that she is 100% Lisa. A person who speaks authentically and from the heart. A woman who owns her personal power and has been able to use it to translate her unique brand of game changer thinking to take on the world."
TAREN HOCKING – FOUNDER, SUSTAINING WOMEN IN BUSINESS

ACKNOWLEDGEMENTS

Massive thanks to my incredible team who love and support me every single day to be the best version of myself. Big shout out to the core team – Claire, Mel, Mel D, Jade, Jess, Edie, Tara, Tia, Lila, Phoebe, Anita, Lisa D, Hannah, Michelle, Nina, Kate, Bec, Sam.

Big shout out to Amy and Mel for helping me to structure my thoughts and pull out the best in me. To Jade and Edie for putting my vision perfectly on the page. And to Claire and Jodes for securing the most extraordinary distribution and working with me to really make these babies move and find a big place in this world. You are all incredible and helped make this book happen at an extraordinary and alarming pace – we certainly don't do things by halves and I love having you all by my side on this crazy, fast-paced, high-growth journey.

Our extended team of 37+ distributors and roughly 70 writers around the globe. A special mention goes out to Jodie Frazer, Shayne McNally, Trevor West, Scott Snodgrass, Janet Judge, Dennis Jones, Victoria Harper, Hunter Drinan and Warren Broom.

Thank you to our incredible readers, who cheer us on and support and inspire me every single day. Thanks to you, the movement is growing and we are inspiring positive change in this world.

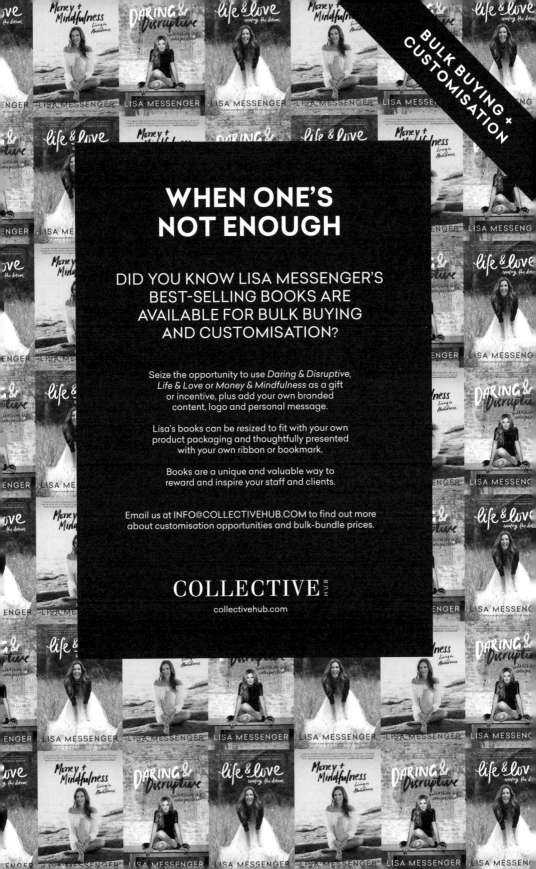

COLLECTIVE HUB

Collective Hub is a global community of entrepreneurial and creative minds who have an appetite for challenging the status quo – they are the game changers, rule breakers, thought leaders and style makers. The movement began with *The Collective*, a monthly design and lifestyle magazine distributed in 37 countries, and whether you are looking for a new idea to tackle, business advice from industry professionals or a friendly dose of encouragement, *The Collective* is your guide to making an impact in this world. Since then, the international Collective Hub community has grown to encompass events, collaborations, strategic partnerships, an ambassador program and various online hubs – all echoing the same philosophies created within our pages.

COLLECTIVEHUB.COM 🅕 🅨 🅞

@lisamessenger #moneyandmindfulness @collectivehub #collectivehub

SHOP / EVENTS / STORIES + MORE

COLLECTIVEHUB.COM

COLLECT THEM ALL

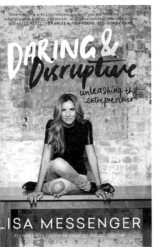

COLLECTIVEHUB.COM